Final Cut Pro®

PORTABLE GENIUS

Final Cut Pro®

PORTABLE GENIUS

by GeniusDV

WILEY

Wiley Publishing, Inc.

Final Cut Pro® Portable Genius

Published by
Wiley Publishing, Inc.
10475 Crosspoint Blvd.
Indianapolis, IN 46256
www.wiley.com

For general information on our other products and services or to obtain technical support, please contact our Customer Care Department within the U.S. at (800) 762-2974, outside the U.S. at (317) 572-3993 or fax (317) 572-4002.

Wiley also publishes its books in a variety of electronic formats. Some content that appears in print may not be available in electronic books.

Library of Congress Control Number: 2008933077

WILEY

About the Author

John Lynn is co-owner of GeniusDV, a digital video training center, headquartered in Orlando. His background includes working as a systems integrator delivering and installing high-end broadcast equipment. John has worked on a variety of national television shows, including *Curt Gowdy's Outdoor World*. His passion for teaching has led him around the country teaching film and video editing. NASA, Lockheed Martin, MTV, and the U.S. Army have praised his training expertise. John is one of very few active certified Final Cut Pro and Avid instructors. He also holds an MFA from the Florida State University Film School.

Credits

Senior Acquisitions Editor
Stephanie McComb

Project Editor
Chris Wolfgang

Technical Editor
Jeff Fortune

Copy Editor
Marylouise Wiack

Editorial Manager
Robyn B. Siesky

Vice President & Group Executive Publisher
Richard Swadley

Vice President & Publisher
Barry Pruett

Business Manager
Amy Knies

Senior Marketing Manager
Sandy Smith

Project Coordinator
Erin Smith

Graphics and Production Specialists
Beth Brooks
Jennifer Henry
Andrea Hornberger

Quality Control Technician
Melissa Bronnenberg

Proofreading
Broccoli Information Management

Indexing
Sherry Massey

To Betsi Green, my first student, and biggest fan.
Always and forever.

Acknowledgments

First and foremost, I would like to thank my parents, John and Lorraine Lynn, for their continued support in pursuing my dream as an educator. I never would have made it to this point without you.

Thanks to the staff at GeniusDV, including Mike Willats and Jeff Fortune, for the inspiration and excitement to drive forward. Your fresh ideas and suggestions really made this book exciting to write. Also, a special thanks to all of our instructors, in particular Paul Sulsky who helped contribute his thoughts and content to this book.

Sincere appreciation goes to Chris Wolfgang and Stephanie McComb, my project editor and acquisitions editor, respectively. Thank you both for putting up with me through the whole process and for being so good to me from start to finish.

Thanks and salutations go to my technical editor, Jeff Fortune, for his expertise and brilliant suggestions. Special thanks to Sarah Willgrube for helping assisting with technical editing.

Special thanks to the folks at the Jacksonville Fire and Rescue Dept for use of their footage. Thank you, Jaime Gomez, for the use of the incredible still images.

Contents

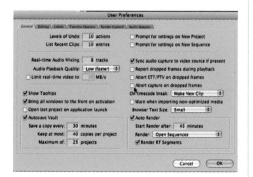

chapter 4

Which Editing Technique Fits My Style?   60

chapter 5

How Do I Use Final Cut Pro as a Professional Sound and Mixing Tool?   78

chapter 6

Which Title Tool Should I Use?   100

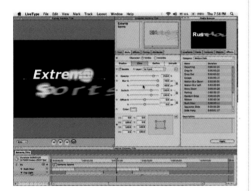

chapter 7

How Can I Use Final Cut Pro for High-End Effects Compositing?   128

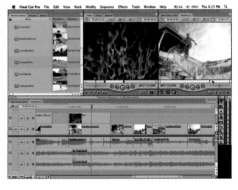

chapter 8

Can I Use Final Cut Pro to Produce Complex Motion Effects? 146

How Many Ways Can I Use Filters? 168

chapter 10

How Can I Maximize the Output
of My Final Cut Pro Product?   200

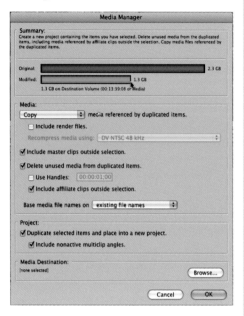

Introduction

Final Cut Pro Portable Genius is designed for those who are familiar with Final Cut Pro but are looking to take their editing skills to the next level. That being said, a novice will still greatly benefit from reading this book.

Final Cut Pro Portable Genius does follow a certain workflow that will help those with limited experience, but each chapter is designed to hold up on its own in terms of the concepts and ideas that are covered.

Let's face it, most of us have learned Final Cut Pro on our own time, and we have learned it by playing around with the features that make sense to our workflow. Hence, some topics help introduce some solid techniques that you may have missed as you've learned the software on your own. Other topics covered are a bit geeky and meant to help those seasoned users fill in some of the blanks that they've always wondered about.

Bottom line, this book will prove to be invaluable for Final Cut Pro users of all experience levels. It cuts through much of the fluff and traditional techniques you may find in other Final Cut Pro books.

What is Final Cut Pro?

Final Cut Pro is a software product included with a suite of applications called Final Cut Studio. Apple has spent a great deal of time integrating these applications (such as Soundtrack Pro covered in chapter 5, and LiveType, covered in chapter 6) so they communicate well with each other. These combined applications are a critical component of making the most out of Final Cut Pro.

For those new to Final Cut Pro

If you are new to Final Cut Pro, I recommend that you read through the entire first chapter. Afterward, it may be worth skipping over to chapter 3, which deals with importing media. In particular, pay close attention to settings that deal with your DV camera settings. Yes, that's right! There are important settings that pertain to your DV camera even before you begin to launch the Final Cut Pro software.

Experienced Final Cut Pro users

If you've been using Final Cut Pro on a daily basis, you may want to jump right into the more in-depth chapters that pertain to specific items of interest. The meat of the book is in chapters 4 through 9, which focus on exciting editing techniques and effects.

Rather than explaining every Final Cut Pro tool and function, this book is about using the most useful Final Cut Pro functions and employing the most efficient techniques to produce something in the quickest way with the most quality. Enjoy!

What Should My Mac Preferences Be?

There are several settings you should check before you begin capturing and editing. This includes setting up your Mac OS X preferences, a particular necessity before you begin capturing your video.

Check Your Mac OS X Preferences

It's important to check the Mac OS X preferences before launching Final Cut Pro. With Mac OS X, you can disable the energy saving settings that can cause you problems. For example, if your computer is in the middle of a long rendering process, you may not want it to fall asleep. There are other settings that may interfere with Final Cut Pro, such as for Exposé and the Dock.

Configuring the Energy Saver

To configure the Energy Saver preferences with Mac OS X, navigate to the Apple Menu⇨System Preferences. The System Preferences window appears. Click the Energy Saver preferences icon.

I recommend that you set the sleep mode to Never. Of course, allowing your monitor to sleep is not known to have any adverse effects, so you can leave the monitor sleep setting at your individual preference.

There is a check box in the Energy Savings settings that will allow external hard drives to go to sleep when not in use (see figure 1.1). For the purpose of video editing, you don't want to have this box checked. If you allow your hard drives to go to sleep while editing, Final Cut Pro may temporarily lock up while the drives spin up again.

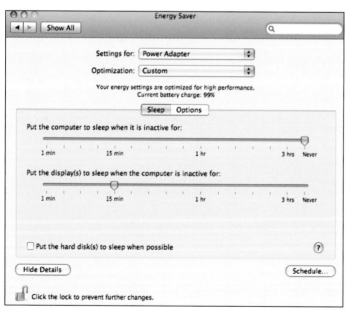

1.1 Energy Saver preferences.

Exposé settings

Exposé is a function within Mac OS X that provides easy access to application windows, the Desktop, the Dashboard, and the screen saver. The Exposé feature can be a useful tool, but it tends to conflict with the applications within the Final Cut Studio, which make use of the entire workspace of your monitor. It is very easy to accidentally activate the Exposé function when working too close to the corners of your screen. This can become annoying. You can avoid this by deactivating the active screen's corners (or *hot corners*) within the Exposé preferences window.

To access the Exposé settings, navigate to the Apple menu⇨System Preferences. Click the Exposé preferences icon. The Exposé dialog box appears, where you can make adjustments to the parameters (see figure 1.2).

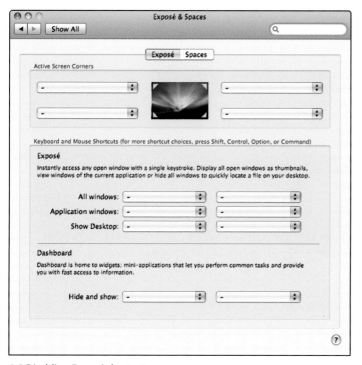

1.2 Disabling Exposé shortcuts.

The hot keys F9 to F11 that are configured within Exposé interfere with the Insert, Overwrite, and Replace key commands within Final Cut Pro. When there is a conflict over the same key, Exposé overrides the Final Cut Pro commands. Either the Exposé or the Final Cut Pro functions can be reassigned, and you are much more likely to use the assigned Final Cut Pro functions than Exposé. Plus, there are specialized keyboards for Final Cut Pro that have the Final Cut Pro functions printed right on their keys. Therefore, you'll definitely want to change those functions that do not match the keyboard. To disable the active screen corners and Exposé functions, use the drop-down menu for each parameter and select a dash (-) to disable the function.

Turning off the Dashboard

The Dashboard is a pop-up window that provides access to mini-applications called widgets. Although this is a great feature, the Dashboard is assigned to the same key as the Superimpose feature of Final Cut Pro, which is F12. I recommend that you assign the Dashboard to a different function key or keep the Dashboard in the Dock, which should be adequate to use this feature.

Configuring the Mighty Mouse

At first glance, the Apple Mighty Mouse appears to only have one button, but in fact, it is right- and left-sensitive. There is also a scroll ball in the middle of the mouse, which also functions as a button by depressing the scroll wheel ball. In addition to the right and left buttons, the Mighty Mouse has two additional touch-sensitive areas on the top of both sides of the mouse (see figure 1.3). These touch-sensitive areas only require that you tap on one side of the mouse to activate a particular function.

You can configure the Mighty Mouse to have as many as four different functions. Navigate to the Apple menu⇨System Preferences, click the Keyboard & Mouse preferences icon, and click the Mouse tab. This is where you can assign functions to all of the mouse areas (see figure 1.3).

Throughout this book, I will refer to *right clicking*, which refers to clicking on the right side of the Mighty Mouse, or its secondary button. Final Cut Pro makes extensive use of right clicking on various items within the interface. If you are using your Mac for the very first time, the default configuration for the Mighty Mouse has both sides of the mouse configured as the primary button. It is extremely important to configure the right side of the Mighty Mouse as the secondary button. Otherwise, the Mighty Mouse will only function as a single button mouse.

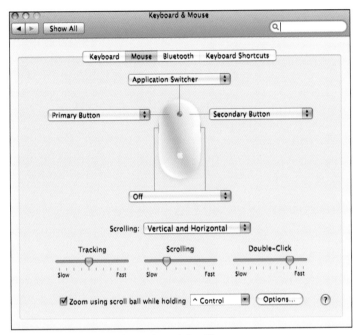

1.3 System preferences for Apple's Mighty Mouse.

Some users simply don't like using the Mighty Mouse. Fortunately, you can use any third-party USB mouse with Final Cut Pro. Just plug in the third-party mouse, and it will automatically work.

Genius

If you have a third-party mouse that has a mouse wheel, you cannot configure the mouse wheel as a third button. The menu options to configure the mouse wheel disappear when your Mac does not detect a Mighty Mouse. However, you can trick the Mac OS X into configuring the wheel by plugging in your old Mighty Mouse first and then configuring the mouse settings. Unplug the Mighty Mouse, and you can continue to use your third-party mouse with the mouse wheel configured as a third button.

Video editing can require a very precise touch. Having your tracking speed calibrated to your individual comfort level is very important. You can also adjust the Tracking slider within the Keyboard and Mouse preferences until you have a comfortable tracking speed. With the same mentality as adjusting the tracking speed, you can adjust your Double-Click speed.

Disabling software updates

Software updates are very important but can cause problems if you are in the middle of a project. In the System Preferences of your Mac, you can assign the frequency at which your Mac checks for software updates. Your Mac needs to be connected to the Internet for this to work properly.

Caution

Consider waiting until you finish a Final Cut Pro project before installing updates to Final Cut Pro.

Adjust Spotlight settings for finding media and sound elements

You can use the Spotlight feature to search for files to use in a Final Cut Studio project. For example, I often use it to search for sound effects, telling Spotlight to only search for audio files. This causes the search to go more quickly and display more manageable results.

Genius

Because Final Cut Studio installs thousands of Soundtrack Pro audio files, you already have an extensive music and sound effects library sitting on your hard drive. If you configure Spotlight to only search for audio files, you will have easy access to those files directly within a Finder window. This provides an easy way to import those files directly into Final Cut Pro.

To configure Spotlight preferences, follow these steps:

1. **Click the search icon in the upper-right corner of the Mac OS X menu bar.** Or, you can use the keyboard shortcut ⌘+Space bar.

2. **Type a word into the spotlight search field.** For example, type the word **camera shutter.** Available files containing the search word *camera shutter* appear within the search list.

3. **At the bottom of the search list, click the Spotlight Preferences (see figure 1.4).** Configure the Spotlight preferences to only search for music.

4. **Go back and redo your search.** This time, only music files that contain the word *camera shutter* appear within the search results.

5. **Click Show All at the top of the search list to reveal the relevant items within a separate Finder window.**

Configuring the character map

The character map is a critical function that you'll frequently use with Final Cut Pro. It is part of the International settings within the System Preferences (see figure 1.5). The character map allows you to copy and paste characters that are not readily available within each font set. In some cases, it's almost like having a miniature clip art library of various symbols and icons. Common uses include the copyright symbol, trademark symbol, or languages that require the tilde symbol above a particular letter. You can find all these elements within the Character Palette.

Genius You can use the character map to place shapes and various clip art into programs like LiveType or Apple Motion. You can further manipulate these shapes to create special effects.

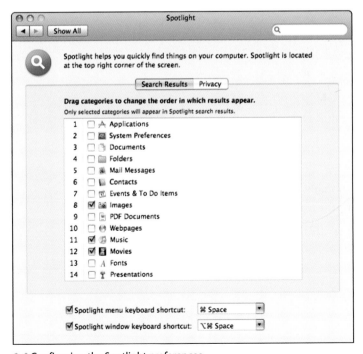

1.4 Configuring the Spotlight preferences.

1.5 The character map.

To configure the character map, follow these steps:

1. **Click the International icon within the System Preferences.**

2. **Click the Input Menu tab at the top.**

3. **Place a check mark for the Character Palette option.**

4. **Place a check mark for the Show input menu in menu bar option, which is located at the bottom of the dialog.**

When you are finished with these steps, you should notice a flag in the upper-right corner of the Finder's menu bar. Doing this allows you to use the Character Palette by right-clicking the flag on the menu bar (see figure 1.6).

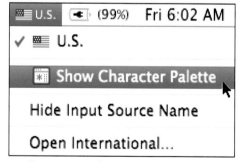

1.6 Character map flag at the top of the Finder menu bar.

Using a MobileMe account

If you are not familiar with MobileMe, it is a service provided by Apple that allows you to publish a Web site and share files. You can configure a MobileMe account by clicking on the MobileMe icon within the System Preferences dialog box. Type in your MobileMe username and password to sign in. If you do not have a MobileMe account click on the Learn More button within the dialog box for a free trial or to sign up.

Configuring the iDisk

The iDisc allows you to easily share files with others through your MobileMe account. After you are signed into your account, you can configure your iDisk by clicking in the iDisk tab within the MobileMe dialog window (see figure 1.7). Click on the Start button to sync the iDisk and an iDisk icon appears on your desktop.

Genius

If you have multiple Macs synchronized to the same MobileMe account, you can simply drag a file into your iDisk, and it becomes available to be dragged off the iDisk of another Mac synchronized to the same MobileMe account.

1.7 Configuring and syncing the iDisk.

Think of the iDisk as an Internet-based jump drive that you can use to transfer files. The iDisk functions just like a regular disk drive where you can add or remove files. From a practical point of view, the iDisk provides an easy way for you to send and receive files from other individuals. Quite often, you may need to send copies of your finished product to someone over the Internet. The iDisk makes this process very easy.

Caution Since the iDisk is a remote disk drive that uses the Internet for storing files, the transfer process for large files can be slow.

Configuring the Dock

The Dock is an area where aliases to various applications may be stored. By default, it is located at the bottom of the screen. This tends to interfere with Final Cut Pro when attempting to navigate within the Timeline window. I recommend that you position the Dock off to the right-hand side of the screen (see figure 1.8), where it will be out of the way of critical interface windows.

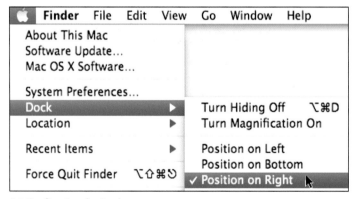

1.8 Configuring the Dock.

Hardware Configuration

Inspecting and understanding how your hardware is configured is very important. This is particularly critical when you make additional purchasing decisions pertaining to new peripherals such as hard drives, cameras, tape machines, and transport devices.

Video-editing keyboard

One of the best things that you can do for your editing development is to purchase a video-editing keyboard (see figure 1.9). Video-editing keyboards have the functions of every key printed right on them. Many also display the icon that represents the function on the key. There are also overlays available that can be placed over a standard keyboard.

1.9 A video-editing keyboard.

Research storage options

The specifications of different external storage devices can play a big role in deciding which one is best for you. The three main specifications to consider are size, speed, and interface.

With storage having gone from over a $1,000 per gigabyte 12 years ago, to as little as 30 cents in 2008, it is much easier to allocate additional space for a project. You have the choice of using separate storage devices for each project or going with a larger drive for multiple projects. Terabyte external hard drives have become rather common.

The next specification to consider is the speed at which the drive spins. Drives with speeds of 5400rpm, 7200rpm, 10,000rpm, and even 15,000rpm are available. There is a direct association between hard drive speed and processor performance. This isn't hard to believe because the faster the drive spins, the faster the processor is able to read from it.

The last specification to consider is the interface. The way that your drive is connected to the computer affects its performance. The most common interface types are FireWire, USB 2.0, and serial ATA.

Cable length limitations

It is important to realize that there are cable length limitations. Table 1.1 shows the various limitations for each type of connection. Longer cables can cause a variety of problems when you're working with digital video. Extremely long FireWire cables simply will not work when transferring data from your DV camera into Final Cut Pro. In my experience, anything over 6 feet doesn't perform properly. The shorter the cable, the better off you are.

Table 1.1 Commonly Used Connections on Storage Devices

Connection	Max Speed	Max Devices	Max Cable Length
USB 1.1	1.5MB/s	1 device per connector	5m
USB 2.0	60MB/s	1 device per connector	5m
FireWire 400	50MB/s	63	4.5m
FireWire 800	100MB/s	63	4.5m
Serial ATA (SATA 1)	150MB/s	1 device per connector	2m
Serial ATA (SATA 2)	300MB/s	1 device per connector	2m
SCSI Ultra-320	320MB/s	16	12m

Shielding on cables

The shielding on cables is very important, particularly when dealing with FireWire cables. Less-expensive cables may only have a small amount of shielding. A bad FireWire cable will act like an antenna and pick up all sorts of rogue transmission signals.

In some cases, this interference can become embedded into your digital video clips during the transferring process. You certainly wouldn't want to end up with a conversation between two truck drivers in the middle of your imported video. Use cables that have a heavy wire shielding that is visible beneath the rubber coating.

FireWire devices

FireWire is also known as IEEE 1394. FireWire 400 transfers at a data rate of close to 50 MB per second. When using the Log and Capture tool within Final Cut Pro, you must use a FireWire cable to capture media. Most video cameras and decks attach to drives and computers through a 4-pin to

6-pin FireWire cable. When dealing with a camera or deck that uses a 6-pin to 6-pin cable, you want to be careful, because those extra two pins carry current.

FireWire 800, also known as IEEE1394b, transfers at a data rate of close to 100 megabytes per second. Whenever possible, you should certainly choose a FireWire 800 connection over a FireWire 400 connection. Most modern hard drives have connections for both.

One advantage of using FireWire devices is that you can loop them together. You can chain up 63 devices together that all connect to just one FireWire port. Other devices that use USB or Serial ATA connections require a separate port for each device.

Caution

If you loop a FireWire 800 device through a FireWire 400 device, the entire chain only runs at 400Mb/s.

Caution

If a USB 2.0 device is hooked into a USB 1.1 device, (for example, by plugging into a port on the keyboard or monitor) the USB 2.0 device will be limited to the speed of the USB 1.1 device.

USB devices

USB has two speeds: USB 1.0 and USB 2.0. Technically speaking, USB 1.0 has been replaced with USB 1.1 to rectify early problems with USB 1.0. Both specifications use the exact same cable. USB1.1 is designed for low-power devices, such as a mouse or a keyboard. Some jump drives work in a USB 1.1 port, but with a very slow data transfer rate.

USB 2.0 drives support a data rate of 60MB per second. In general, USB drives are cheaper than drives that have FireWire 400/800 connections. The one drawback of USB devices is that you cannot loop them together in a chain; each USB device requires its own dedicated connection. This is problematic if you are editing on a MacBook Pro, because of the limited number of USB ports.

Serial ATA devices

External serial ATA devices are relatively new to the marketplace. Before purchasing one of these drives, make sure your computer has an external serial ATA connector to accept this type of drive. Otherwise, you may need to invest in a serial ATA card that provides the necessary interface connection.

What are some critical camera settings?

Before you begin editing, make sure your camera settings are correct. This is particularly important when it comes to setting audio data rates and video frame rates within the camera.

1.10 Setting the audio bit rate in a camera.

Audio bit rate

It is important to set the audio to 16 bit in order to achieve 48 kHz audio. Most cameras are preset to record with 12-bit audio, so this is a setting you will most likely have to change (see figure 1.10). If 12-bit audio is imported into Final Cut Pro, there is a chance that the video clips will drift out of sync from the audio clips on sequences that exceed 3 minutes.

Video frame rate

Take note of the video format setting in your camera. The most popular formats include DV and HDV. Also take note of the frame rate. Popular frame rates for North American users include 29.97 and 24p. For European users, 25 fps is the standard frame rate.

Caution

In order to correctly capture footage, it is important that you match the Audio/Video Settings within Final Cut Pro to the correct format you are ingesting.

To configure the capture settings for Final Cut Pro, navigate to the Final Cut Pro menu ⇨ Audio/Video Settings. The Audio/Video Settings dialog appears. You can adjust the capture preset by using the Capture Preset drop-down menu. Select the appropriate preset that matches the video format you have recorded.

If you are receiving media from a third party, it is sometimes difficult to figure out which video format was used to record the footage. There are over 80 different video presets within Final Cut Pro! Fortunately, if you configure the Easy Setup preferences (see figure 1.11) to use (all formats), and (all rates), Final Cut Pro will automatically adjust your sequence settings to the first clip that is edited to the timeline.

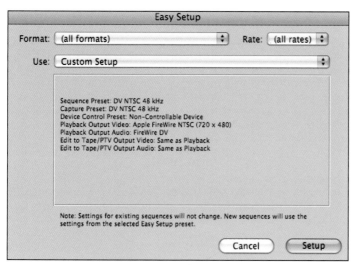

1.11 Configuring Easy Setup.

For more information on how to record or ingest media into Final Cut Studio, refer to Chapter 3.

Final Cut Studio Installation Options

Final Cut Studio is a massive install, requiring 59GB of space to install all the applications! This can be problematic for laptop users.

Caution

The Final Cut Studio software package ships with eight DVDs that contain all the install files. Installation can take up to three hours, and then you need to install all of the available Final Cut Studio updates.

When installing Final Cut Studio, you may want to deselect some options if you do not plan on using them. For example, you may not want to install Cinema Tools if you are not producing physical motion picture film prints.

The files that take up the most space are the Soundtrack Pro music loops, Motion media, and LiveType media. If you are limited on disk space, you may want to consider deselecting these items (see figure 1.12).

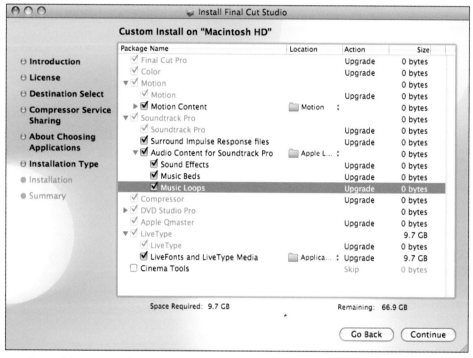

1.12 Customizing your Final Cut Studio installation.

Genius

If you are installing Final Cut Studio onto several computers or workstations, you may want to create disk images of the Final Cut Studio installation DVDs. Installing Final Cut Studio from a disk image will install the entire program in about 45 minutes. Also, you won't have to sit and switch out individual disks. As long as all the disk images have been mounted, the install will proceed all the way through to the end.

To create a disk image, follow these steps:

1. **Launch the Disk Utility program.** This utility is found within Mac HD⇨Applications⇨Utilities⇨Disk Utility.

2. **Insert the first installation disk for Final Cut Studio.** The Installation disk appears on the left side of the Disk Utility window. Highlight the disk.

3. **Click the New Image button (see figure 1.13).** Choose a location to save the disk image.

4. **Repeat this step for each of the installation disks.** If you have extra space on your hard drive, change the image format to read/write instead of compressed. This increases the speed of installing the files from a disk image because they are not compressed.

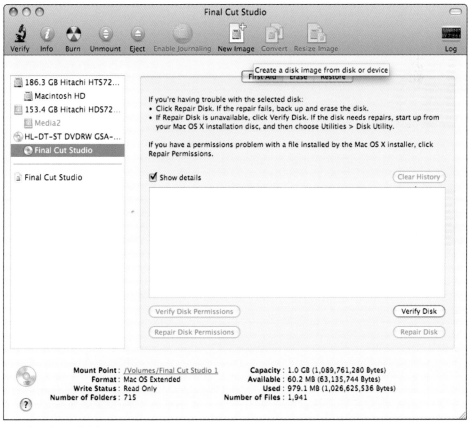

1.13 Creating a disk image.

It will take awhile to create all the disk images. Once the disk images are saved to your hard drive (see figure 1.14), you can take them to another computer, and the entire installation process will move much faster.

To install Final Cut Studio from a set of disk images, follow these steps:

1. **Double-click each disk image.** You'll repeat this step eight times. I recommend skipping the verification process. This mounts eight virtual disks to the Mac OS X desktop.

2. **Open the first disk image, which should be from the first Final Cut Studio disk.** Double-click the Install Final Cut Studio icon.

After installing Final Cut Studio for the first time, it is important that you check for additional updates. You will need to check for updates more than once to complete the entire update process. Generally, the first time you perform an update, you will see a pro applications updater. Run the update a second time to reveal the updates for each Final Cut Studio application.

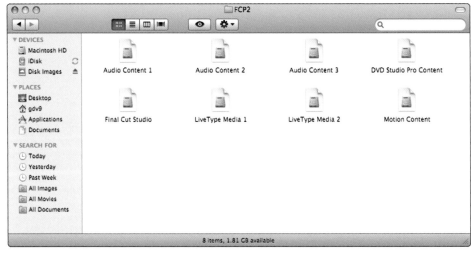

1.14 Mounted disk images.

Caution Although it's important to update the Final Cut Studio software, I do not recommend updating the software while you are in the middle of a job. Always finish any critical jobs before performing the update process.

To run the software update, navigate to the Apple menu⇨Software Updates. Then check the updates that you want to install.

Troubleshooting Final Cut Pro Hardware Problems

Troubleshooting problems can be a frustrating experience. Here is a short list of common problems that you may experience and how to solve them.

Check your cables

If you are experiencing problems capturing video, always check the cables that connect your tape machine to Final Cut Pro. Most users will be using a FireWire cable that connects directly from the tape machine to the computer. Defective FireWire cables can wreak havoc on the capturing process.

Deleting the Final Cut Pro preferences file

A common fix for unexplained issues relating to Final Cut Pro is to delete the Final Cut Pro preferences file. For example, let's say that your system is working perfectly fine one day, and then you come in to the office the next morning to find that Final Cut Pro will not capture anything. It's possible that the Final Cut Pro preferences file has become corrupted. You can find the Final Cut Pro preferences file at the following location:

Mac HD ⇨ Users ⇨ *Username* ⇨ Library ⇨ Preferences ⇨ Final Cut Pro user data ⇨ Final Cut Pro 6.0 Prefs

If you choose, you can safely delete the entire Final Cut Pro user data folder. Upon relaunching the software, Final Cut Pro automatically rebuilds this entire folder.

Caution

Although deleting the Final Cut Pro preferences file is harmless, it resets any preferences that you have adjusted back to the original default settings. When you launch Final Cut Pro, the software will act like it's a new installation with a new set of default preferences.

Rebuilding permissions

Occasionally, the file permissions within Mac OS X can become corrupted. You can safely rebuild the file permissions using the Disk Utility. The Disk Utility is located in the Mac HD ⇨ Applications ⇨ Utilities folder.

What Are the Critical Final Cut Pro Preferences?

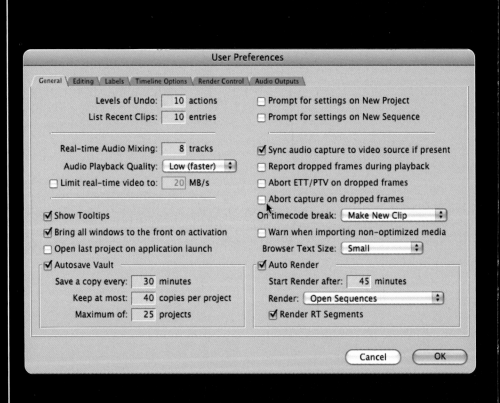

Before you begin editing in Final Cut Pro, you should customize a few preferences to improve your workflow. Because there are many settings and preferences, I'll cover just the critical settings that have an immediate impact on how the software functions.

Working with Multiple User Accounts

Mac OS X allows you to configure your system for multiple users. Depending on your workflow, it may not be necessary to create individual user accounts for your Final Cut Pro editing system. Each Mac OS X user account has its own settings. This means that if you have three people who are going to use the system, you would have three different login IDs (see figure 2.1).

Mac OS X
gdv9

Bob

Jeff

John

Sleep   Restart   Shut Down

2.1 Multiple Mac OS X Login IDs.

Caution

If possible, I recommend working with only one primary Mac OS X user account for Final Cut Pro. Otherwise, each Mac OS X user will have a different set of user preferences. While this doesn't sound like a bad idea, it can cause serious problems if you have different accounts set up to capture media in different locations.

User Preferences

The user preferences can be found under the Final Cut Pro menu⇨User Preferences. A dialog appears with various user preference tabs at the top of the User Preferences window.

Levels of undo

The very first preference is the levels of undo. You should immediately set this to the maximum value of 99. There is really no reason to leave it set to anything less than the maximum value.

Real Time audio mixing

This setting refers to how many tracks of audio Final Cut Pro can play back simultaneously before it sounds a beeping alarm. If you exceed the number of tracks, you will hear a beeping sound when you play through your sequence. The specified number of real-time audio tracks also refers to any audio filters placed within those tracks. For example, if you have four audio tracks with an audio filter on one of the tracks, your real-time audio playback count is now at five. I've found that you can increase this value to 16 without having any problems.

A major factor that comes into play when you have multiple audio tracks is the speed of your hard drive. If you find your system is sluggish when working with multiple audio tracks, consider purchasing a hard drive that has a high RPM value (revolutions per minute). In most cases, 7200 rpm drives are perfectly fine.

Caution

The current MacBook Pros may ship with an internal drive that spins at 5000rpm, which is pushing the limit of the drive to be able to play full motion video.

Audio playback quality

The audio playback quality setting affects how Final Cut Pro deals with mismatched audio sample rates. If you are working with clips that match the sample rate set for your sequence, this setting does not do anything and has no effect on playback quality of the audio.

You should leave the audio playback setting at Low (faster) (see figure 2.2). This setting refers to how Final Cut Pro handles mismatched audio clips that do not conform to your sequence's audio sample rate. In most situations, you will be working with an audio sample rate of 48 kHz.

2.2 Audio playback quality.

If there are other clips mixed within a sequence that are not 48 kHz, Final Cut Pro attempts to convert those audio samples to 48 kHz on the fly. This requires a tremendous amount of processing power, which is why you want to leave the setting at Low (faster). It is best that you convert all of your audio clips to a 48 kHz sample rate before importing them into Final Cut Pro. In that case, this setting doesn't have any effect at all. See Chapter 3 for more information on how to convert audio sample rates to 48 kHz.

Opening last project on application launch

I recommend that you disable this setting, which prevents Final Cut Pro from automatically launching the last set of projects that were previously open. Leaving this setting on can be frustrating if you want to begin a new session. This is because you'll have to sit and wait for Final Cut Pro to load the last project each time you launch the software. Worse yet, if you are in a working environment where you have multiple editors working on different projects, you'll have to wait for the software to load someone else's project. Then you'll have to close their project and load your own.

To combat this problem, I recommend that you do not launch Final Cut Pro from the application icon. Instead, launch Final Cut Pro from the saved project icon (see figure 2.3). This prevents Final Cut Pro from opening someone else's work. Plus, it automatically launches the project that you have double-clicked.

2.3 Final Cut Pro project icon.

Configuring AutoSave

You should always leave the AutoSave vault turned on. I also recommend increasing the number of copies per project and the number of projects that Final Cut Pro will save. These files don't take up a lot of space, so it makes sense to type in a higher value than the default settings.

Caution Final Cut Pro saves separate copies of your entire project to a specified location on a hard drive. In other words, if you do not explicitly save your project, you need to navigate to the AutoSave vault to find the AutoSaved copies. So if you're editing along and the power goes out and you haven't explicitly saved your project, you have to use the AutoSave vault to recover an earlier version.

If you need to access an old version of a project, you can navigate to the AutoSave vault to find a list of all the available projects that have been saved. The default location is Mac HD ⇨ Users ⇨ *Username* ⇨ Documents ⇨ Final Cut Pro Documents ⇨ Autosave Vault ⇨ *Name of Project*

Caution I do not recommend changing the default location of the AutoSave vault. This is especially dangerous if you plan to use multiple Mac OS X accounts. Each Mac OS X user could potentially have a different location for the AutoSave vault.

Assuming your AutoSave preference is enabled, you can use the Restore Project function to recover projects directly from the AutoSave vault. Navigate to the File Menu⇨Restore Project to see the list of available projects that can be recovered.

Abort capture on dropped frames

Be careful with this setting, as changing it really affects your workflow. This setting is all about capturing from tape-based formats. If you have a 60-minute tape and you have a tight deadline, you may not want Final Cut Pro to abort a capture while you are at lunch waiting for a tape to be recorded into the system. You may be better off unchecking this option and allowing Final Cut Pro to continue the capture but warn you that there were potential problems. You can then investigate and recapture any areas that did not capture correctly.

Timecode breaks

Timecode refers to numbers that are assigned to each video frame. For users in North America, timecode is typically measured at 30 fps (frames per second). European users have a counting method of 25 fps. timecode looks like 00:00:00:00, which translates to Hours: Minutes: Seconds: Frames.

Mini-DV cameras automatically start the timecode at 00:00:00:00 each time you start recording onto a new tape. As long as you are parked on an existing frame of video, the mini-DV camera continues the count forward with new timecode numbers each time you start recording again. If you eject the tape and start recording where there is no video image, the timecode numbers reset to 00:00:00:00.

This happens because users are afraid to rewind the tape too far back into a previous video image, and so they fast-forward to where there is no existing footage. This means that it's possible to have one tape with repeating sets of timecode values. This wreaks havoc with nonlinear editing systems, and it is considered a bad practice to have tapes with timecode breaks.

To combat this problem, you can tell Final Cut Pro to either warn after capture or to make a new clip each time it encounters a timecode break. I prefer the latter setting, which creates a new clip each time a timecode break is encountered.

Still freeze duration

Final Cut Pro automatically gives you two minutes of any still image that is imported into the system. Final Cut Pro automatically marks in and out points in the middle of the clip. This is important, because you'll have extra media on both sides of the image if you want to create a transition effect that goes from one image to another.

Under the editing tab within the User Preferences dialog, you see a setting for the Still/Freeze Duration. This tells Final Cut Pro the distance to mark for still images or freeze frames.

Configuring audio outputs

You can configure Final Cut Pro to output as many as 24 independent audio tracks. While this may not seem practical to many of us, it is a fantastic feature for those who work in the motion picture business. This means that you can output a QuickTime movie that contains 24 independent audio channels that are not mixed together. You can use a QuickTime movie to send all of your audio elements to a production facility so it has all of your original audio tracks embedded into one QuickTime movie.

To configure a sequence to output multiple audio tracks within a QuickTime movie, follow these steps:

1. **Find your sequence within the Browser window.**

2. **Right-click the sequence and navigate to settings within the contextual pop-up menu.** A sequence settings dialog appears.

3. **Click the Audio tab within the Sequence settings dialog.**

4. **Change the number of outputs to a maximum value of 24.** Choose a value that matches the number of tracks you plan on having in your final sequence.

5. **Change each set of audio channels to either Stereo or Dual Mono.** In most cases, you assign each set of channels to be dual mono. Music that is in stereo would be an exception. For example, if you plan on having stereo music on channels 7 and 8, you would set that particular pair of channels to stereo. A warning dialog may appear indicating that the current hardware device does not support the number of outputs. If you see this warning dialog, check the Downmix all outputs to Stereo option. Don't worry; you'll still be able to output a QuickTime movie with all the audio tracks separated.

6. **Right-click each audio track and assign the track to its appropriate output.** For the most part, you assign the same sequence tracks to the same output tracks. Figure 2.4 shows a sequence with four audio channel outputs. Each channel must be assigned to its corresponding output.

2.4 Assigning audio tracks to their correct outputs.

7. **Right-click your sequence within the Browser window and choose Export⇨QuickTime Movie from the contextual pop-up menu.**

You now have a QuickTime movie with up to 24 independent audio tracks. You can verify this for yourself by importing the QuickTime movie back into Final Cut Pro.

System Settings

The system settings within Final Cut Pro primarily deal with playback control and storage locations for media and the AutoSave vault. The System Preferences are located under the Final Cut Pro menu ⇨ System Settings.

Setting the scratch disks

The term *scratch disk* refers to a location where media files are going to be stored. The default location for the scratch disk is set to Mac HD ⇨ Users ⇨ *Username* ⇨ Documents ⇨ Final Cut Pro documents.

You can set the scratch disk by clicking the Scratch Disks tab at the top of the System Settings window. I recommend changing the scratch disk location to the root level of an external drive.

Caution

The default location of the scratch disk is on the internal drive. It's certainly not a good idea to record media to your internal drive. DV media requires a lot of storage, and you will quickly exceed the capacity of your internal drive if you continue to record media to it.

Limiting capture time

You can limit the amount of time Final Cut Pro captures when using the Capture Now feature. This is a cool feature if you plan on leaving your system during a capture process and you want Final Cut Pro to stop capturing after a specified amount of time.

To use this feature, Final Cut Pro must preallocate the amount of size needed for the number of minutes specified. If you have enough storage to record only a portion of the amount specified, Final Cut Pro generates an error saying there is insufficient hard drive space. Therefore, make certain that you have more than enough storage to preallocate before you limit the capture time.

Using external editors

An external editor refers to a third-party program that is used outside of Final Cut Pro. You can configure third-party programs to process still image files, video files, and audio files. Once they have been configured, you can send these file types directly to a third-party application without having to leave the Final Cut Pro application. When you are finished editing the file within the third-party application, the file automatically links back to a Final Cut Pro sequence.

An excellent choice might be to configure Adobe Photoshop as an external editor for opening still images. This means you can open still images in Adobe Photoshop directly from a Final Cut Pro sequence.

After you've configured an external editor, follow these steps to open a file directly from a Final Cut Pro sequence:

1. **Right-click a still image within a Final Cut Pro sequence.**

2. **Select Open in Editor from the contextual pop-up menu (see figure 2.5).** The file automatically opens within the specified external editor.

Caution

Photoshop PSD files operate differently when you open them within an external editor. When you import a PSD file into Final Cut Pro, Final Cut Pro creates a nested sequence from the file instead of a graphic. You need to double-click the nested sequence to gain access to the Photoshop layers first. From that point, it doesn't matter which Photoshop layer you open; they all point to the same file.

3. **When you finish with the file, make sure you save it within your third-party application.** This automatically updates the Final Cut Pro sequence.

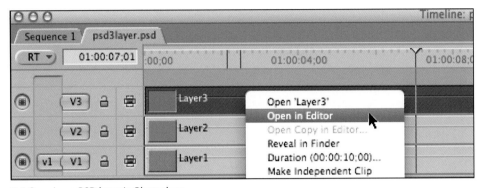

2.5 Opening a PSD layer in Photoshop.

Audio/Video Settings

You can find the Audio and Video settings by navigating to the Final Cut Pro menu ➪ System Settings. The audio and video preferences can be confusing, as there are over 80 sequence presets and 30 capture presets!

Caution

It is very important that you match the capture preset to the type of media that you have recorded onto tape. Otherwise, you will be unable to ingest the media from a deck or camera. The most common consumer formats are DV-NTSC, DV-PAL, and HDV. Because Final Cut Pro is also used by high-end professionals, there are also a variety of professional formats within the Capture Preset menu.

Table 2.1 Commonly Used Video Formats

Video Format	Country of Origin	Standard Frame Rate
DV-NTSC	North America	24p, 29.97
PAL	Western Europe	25
HDV	Nonapplicable	24p, 25, 30, 50, 60

Keep in mind that there are many more formats than what is listed in Table 2.1. All that's really important is that you take note of the format that you are shooting with so that you can match your Final Cut Pro capture settings to the same video format.

Genius

The latest version of Final Cut Pro automatically conforms the sequence to match the settings of the first clip that you edit to a sequence. As long as your first clip has been captured correctly, Final Cut Pro will handle everything for you.

If you are ingesting media from tape, you can configure Final Cut Pro to control your camera or tape machine. This means that you have functionality to play, fast-forward, and rewind your tape directly within the Log and Capture window. This also means that you have the opportunity to mark clips prior to capturing the media. For more information on how to log and capture, see Chapter 3.

Connecting a camera or tape machine to your system with a FireWire cable provides deck control. However, controlling a camera or deck through the FireWire cable isn't always the best solution. Because the same FireWire cable is responsible for transferring the video signal, the playback controls are often sluggish and slow to respond to the commands.

High-end professional tape machines may have a connection on the back called a 9-pin serial connection. You can buy an adapter that converts this 9-pin serial connection to a USB serial connection. This provides much better deck control if you configure your system to use it. There are several companies that make 9-pin to USB serial adapters. One company that comes to mind is Keyspan.

Genius

A standard 9-pin serial to USB adapter will not work. You need something called an RS-422 to standard serial adapter. It looks exactly the same as a standard adapter, but it is wired differently.

In addition to this adapter, you'll also need a MiniDin8 serial to DB9 male serial cable in order to connect to a deck that supports 9-pin RS-422 control.

Final Cut Pro users who are using a high-end professional tape machine may require an AJA or Blackmagic I/O box. These devices provide the necessary connections to connect to high-end industrial tape machines. An important item on these break-out boxes is that they have a built-in RS-422 connector, which means you won't need an adapter. You can use a standard DB9 male to DB9 female cable that connects directly from your tape machine into the AJA or Blackmagic I/O box.

After you've installed the adapter, you need to install the manufacturer's software to make it work. When you are finished, click the Capture Settings tab within the Audio/Video settings window to select the RS-422 serial control device (see figure 2.6). When using professional tape machines that support RS-422 control through 9-pin, make sure the tape machine is set to remote. This switch is typically on the front of the machine.

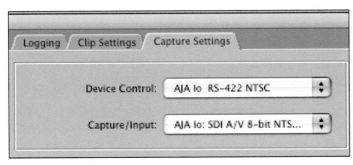

2.6 Device Control menu.

Using Easy Setup

Fortunately, there is an easy setup feature that may save you from having to navigate through all the various Audio and Video settings. Navigate to the Final Cut Pro menu⇨Easy Setup. You still need to specify which format Final Cut Pro uses, but Final Cut Pro will handle everything else.

I recommend leaving the Format option set to (all formats) and the Rate set to (all rates). Some of the common formats are DV–NTSC, DVD–PAL, and HDV. You still need to double-check which video format you have recorded to tape to ensure that you'll be able to ingest the media correctly.

Customizing the Interface

Customizing the Final Cut Pro interface is an integral part of being efficient with the software. You can customize your keyboard shortcuts, window layouts, browser columns, and button wells. After you become accustomed to a particular layout, you can save each layout to a specified file.

Button wells

A button well is a place where you can store shortcut buttons to perform certain tasks. All the major interface windows have button wells. For starters, the timeline window already has two buttons located inside its button well. These are the linked selection and snapping buttons.

Adding buttons to specific button wells is a fantastic way to improve your editing efficiency. For example, instead of having to remember the shortcut for creating a freeze frame, you could map the Make Freeze Frame button to a well (see figure 2.7). Then all you need to do is click the button to create a freeze frame. Any editing function within Final Cut Pro has a corresponding button that you can drag into a button well.

2.7 Make Freeze Frame button added to a button well in the Timeline window.

You can find a list of buttons by navigating to the Tools menu⇨Button List. A Button List dialog appears, breaking down all the available buttons into categories.

Use the search function in the upper-right corner of the Button List dialog to find corresponding buttons. Type the first couple of letters of the function you are looking for into the search field. For example, to find a button for creating a Freeze Frame, you only need to type the letters **fre** and you immediately see items that contain those associated letters. You can find the Make Freeze Frame button from inside the list (see figure 2.8).

2.8 Search function in the Button List dialog window.

Genius

You can add spacers to separate groups of buttons. You can also assign colors to individual buttons. If you use a lot of buttons for various tasks, organizing and assigning colors really helps an editor to distinguish the differences between all the various buttons.

You can add buttons to any button well by simply dragging a button from the button list into a button well. You can rearrange the buttons by dragging one to a new location, and Final Cut Pro automatically pushes the other buttons over to make room for the new location.

To customize a button well, right-click in the button well area (see figure 2.9). A contextual menu appears with a list of choices where you can add spacers, change colors, remove buttons, and save your button list.

You can also remove a button from a well by simply dragging the button outside the area of its resting place. The button disappears in a puff of smoke.

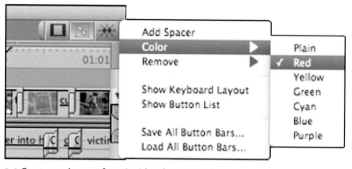

2.9 Contextual menu from inside a button well.

Genius

If you were working in a multi-camera edit, you would want a specific keyboard layout that's geared to multi-camera editing. In fact, Final Cut Pro already has a multi-camera editing keyboard layout designed for you. It's located under the Tools menu ⇨ Keyboard Layout ⇨ Multi-camera editing. Each time you save a new layout, it is available as a new layout under the Keyboard Layout menu.

Keyboard layout

The keyboard is a Final Cut Pro editor's tool of trade. A customized keyboard that's configured with specific shortcuts can save hours of time in an edit session. The well-thought-out keyboard layout can really make a difference in terms of editing workflow.

If you are new to Final Cut Pro, don't be overly concerned about mapping your keyboard. You should be conscious of your editing workflow and habits, and then map your keyboard layout accordingly. This way, you can press a single key instead of navigating through a series of menus. Over time you'll develop your own unique keyboard layout that matches your own unique editing workflow. That's why it's critical that you carry your keyboard layout settings with you at all times.

To customize the keyboard layout, navigate to the Tools menu⇨Keyboard Layout⇨Customize. The default keyboard layout dialog appears (see figure 2.10). You need to unlock the keyboard layout before you can make changes. Click the lock icon that is located in the bottom-left corner of the window to unlock the layout. Find the appropriate shortcut button, and drag the shortcut button onto a key.

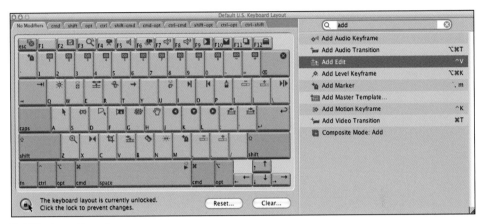

2.10 Keyboard layout.

You'll notice that many of the keys already have keyboard shortcuts applied to them. You can certainly adjust the default settings, but I find most Final Cut Pro editors leave them at the default settings. This is especially true if they own one of those special Final Cut Pro video-editing keyboards, which are designed to match the default layout. If that's the case, you can assign shortcuts that require an additional modifier key such as ⌘+ or shift+.

How Do I Ingest Media into Final Cut Pro?

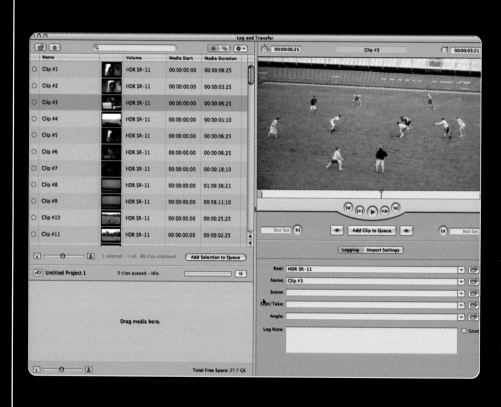

There are two basic ways to get footage into Final Cut Pro: capturing from a video playback deck or camera, or transferring files that have already been recorded to a hard drive or solid-state memory card. The newest forms of tapeless recording can cost less but have additional backup requirements. Cameras being developed now use a tapeless recording method. You can also import still image files, CD audio files, DVD files, and media files obtained from the Internet into Final Cut Pro.

Capturing Media

Capturing is the process used to transfer footage into Final Cut Pro. Each time you capture a clip, Final Cut Pro creates a clip that points to a mediafile. Clips and mediafiles are two separate entities.

A clip appears in the Browser window each time you capture media. It's important to note that the clip doesn't contain the actual media. It is simply a reference to a mediafile that is located on a physical hard drive (see figure 3.1). To keep things organized, Final Cut Pro automatically creates a mediafile based on the name that you give to a clip.

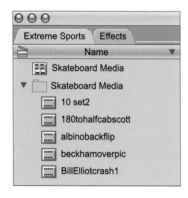

3.1 Clips in the Browser window reference media files on a hard drive.

Unless you've changed the scratch disk preferences within Final Cut Pro, mediafiles are stored in the following default location:

Mac HD ⇨ Users ⇨ *User Name* ⇨ Documents ⇨ Final Cut Pro Documents ⇨ Capture Scratch ⇨ *Name of Project*.

This directory structure seems a bit crazy to me, so I recommend changing the location to the root level of a hard drive. Refer to Chapter 2 to change your system settings.

There are a couple of ways to capture media into Final Cut Pro. These capture methods include the Log and Capture tool and the Log and Transfer tool. They may seem like the same thing, but they function differently.

Log and Capture tool

The Log and Capture tool is used to transfer media from a deck or camera (see figure 3.2). This tool requires that a FireWire cable be connected from the deck or camera into the Macintosh. You can activate it by choosing File menu ⇨ Log and Capture or by using the keyboard shortcut ⌘+8.

Caution

If a deck or camera is not attached and turned on when you start the tool, a message appears that says, "Unable to initialize video deck." If you want to capture footage and you have already opened the Log and Capture tool without having your deck or camera turned on, you need to close the tool, connect and power on the deck or camera, and restart the tool.

3.2 The Log and Capture window.

In the Browser window, look for a small film-clapper icon off in the upper-left corner of the name column. If you do not see one, this means a logging bin has not been set for that particular project. To configure the logging bin, right-click in the gray area of the Name column and select Logging bin from the contextual menu.

After you have specified a logging bin, it is safe to begin capturing. If you have a controllable tape deck or camera connected to your system, you can set in and out points based on timecode values that have been recorded onto your tape. You can set these values using the deck controls and the Log and Capture button in the Log and Capture window. After you have set in and out points (see figure 3.3), press the Capture Clip button. The tape deck or camera then rewinds and captures the clip based on the in and out points that you have marked.

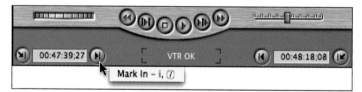

3.3 Setting in and out points in the Log and Capture window.

Genius

With the onslaught of tapeless technologies, and the low cost of hard drives, I recommend that you forget about capturing clips based on timecode and simply ingest the entire tape as one large clip. If this means disabling the deck controls to get the footage in, so be it. You'll also want to tell Final Cut Pro to ignore drop frames while capturing. See Chapter 2 for more information on how to set that up.

Logging

The term *logging* refers to gathering timecode information about particular tapes prior to capturing. At the bottom of the Log and Capture window, you can set in/out points based on timecode values to log a particular clip (see figure 3.4). After you've set in/out points, you should always give your clip a designated Reel number and a description.

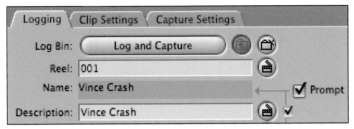

3.4 Logging information within the Log and Capture tool.

It is now okay to click the Log Clip button. This places the clip into the Browser window with a red line through it, indicating the clip is offline. You'll continue this process until you have logged the section of the tape that you need.

When you are finished, highlight your logged clips and press the Batch button at the bottom of the Log and Capture window. Final Cut Pro will do the rest from here. It rewinds your tape machine and begins capturing each clip based on the timecode values entered.

Creating a batch list file

Instead of logging individual clips directly within the Log and Capture tool, you can create a batch list. This method allows someone to create the data needed to make clips without having to run Final Cut Pro. A batch list file is basically an Excel spreadsheet with the columns shown in figure 3.5.

	A	B	C	D	E
1	Name	Media Start	Media End	Reel	Tracks
2	rescuer comes out	00:00:01;13	00:00:11;12	1	1V, 1A
3	interview 4	00:00:02;09	00:00:27;22	1	1V, 1A
4	interview 2	00:00:03;26	00:00:18;11	1	1V, 1A
5	rescuer into hole	00:00:05;29	00:00:15;28	1	1V, 1A
6	hyperbaric chamber	00:29:36;25	00:30:44;05	1	1V, 2A
7	Doctor	00:32:19;04	00:37:00;12	1	1V, 2A
8	Pressure Reading	00:44:46;13	00:44:54;04	1	1V, 2A

3.5 An Excel spreadsheet with required columns for creating clips.

The data from these columns is translated into clips within the Browser window. To import a batch list, choose File menu ⇨ Import ⇨ Batch list. The clips appear in the Browser window with red slashes through them, indicating they have been logged but not captured (see figure 3.6).

To capture the media, highlight the clips and click the Batch button at the bottom of the Log and Capture window. As each clip is captured, the red line disappears, indicating the media has been successfully recorded.

3.6 Offline clips in the Browser window generated from a batch list.

Batch-capturing logged files

After you've logged your files, you still have to capture them using the following steps:

1. **Make sure the deck or camera is turned on and connected.**

2. **Highlight the offline clips within the Browser window.**

3. **Select File ⇨ Batch Capture or press Ctrl+C.**

4. **Confirm the batch capture settings.**

5. **If the tape is not loaded, load it and click Continue on the Insert Reel screen.**

Caution

It is critical that the batch list be accurate. If there are timecode dropouts on the tape, the clips do not capture correctly. It is also critical that you place the correct tape in the tape machine, especially when working with the HDV or mini-DV formats because the timecode on every tape always starts at 00:00:00:00. If you have multiple tapes, they will all have the same set of timecode numbers.

Caution

It is better to cue up the tape a few seconds before the in point instead of after it, because the success rate in capturing missed clips is higher. Final Cut Pro goes into fast forward or fast rewind and completely skips over the end point, continuing to the end of the tape.

Capture Now

The Capture Now feature allows the capture of clips from decks that cannot be controlled by the computer. A good example of this is capturing clips from a VHS deck. VHS tapes don't have a time-code. To capture footage from VHS tapes, the output of the deck is sent to a transcoder, where it converts into a DV signal and feeds into the computer using FireWire.

To capture an entire tape, it's as simple as pressing Play on the tape deck or camera and pressing the Now button at the bottom of the Log and Capture window. The Capture Now feature also allows capturing on the fly for decks that can be controlled by the computer. The process is the same as capturing from a deck that cannot be controlled. Rewind the tape to a point several seconds before you want capture to begin. Start playback and press the Now button in the Log and Capture window.

Capturing without deck control

Based on all the problems that many users may experience with tape-based technologies, it is sometimes necessary to disable the deck controls in order to transfer your footage into Final Cut Pro. To do this, click the Capture Settings tab within the Log and Capture window. You see a menu labeled Device Control. Set the Device Control menu to Non-controllable device. You are now free to capture a live input from whatever signal you feed into Final Cut Pro. At the bottom of the Log and Capture window, you see a Now button. Pressing that button starts the capturing process.

DV Start/Stop Detection

You can create subclips automatically using the start/stop metadata that is embedded in video frames when you start and stop DV format camcorders. Final Cut Pro can place markers in clips at the start and stop locations. This allows you to capture long clips, even whole tapes, and break them up into subclips without logging.

To add markers at the start-and-stop locations for a clip

1. **Select a clip in the Browser or open it in the Viewer.**
2. **Choose Mark ⇨ DV Start/Stop Detect from the Mark menu.**

You now see individual markers in the Viewer window embedded within the clip. These markers represent each time the camera was started and stopped during the recording process (see figure 3.7).

Caution The DV Start/Stop Detection is based on time of day. It requires that you set the time clock within your DV camera. If the clock in your camera is not set, the DV Start/Stop Detection function does not work.

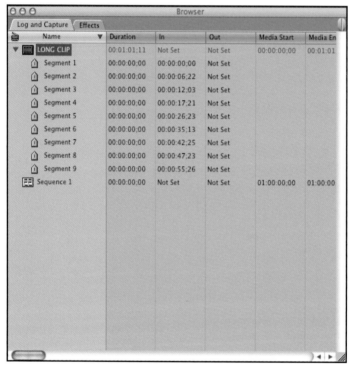

3.7 Embedded markers within a clip in the Viewer window.

The same markers that you see within the Viewer window are also visible within the Browser window. Click the disclosure triangle for the clip containing the markers. Notice that the embedded markers have a duration of zero.

I recommend that you change these markers to subclips before you begin editing. Final Cut Pro measures the distance between each marker, and it uses that information to create subclips (see figure 3.8).

To change markers into subclips:

1. **Highlight all the markers within the clip.**

2. **Choose Modify menu ⇨ Make Subclip.**

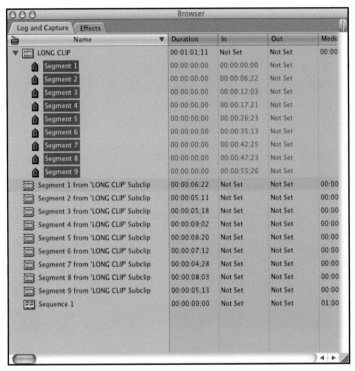

3.8 Markers that have been changed into subclips.

Log and Transfer tool

The Log and Transfer tool allows you to ingest footage from nontape-recording devices such as hard drives, solid-state cards, and optical devices. This tool supports the cameras and formats described in Table 3.1:

49

Table 3.1 Supported Cameras and Formats

Format	Transport Device	Manufacturer
AVCHD	Hard disk, mini-DV, secure digital card, memory stick	All manufacturers
DVCPRO HD	Panasonic P2 card	Panasonic
XDCAM	Optical disk	Sony
Sony Video	Disk Unit devices	Sony

Caution Trying to open the Log and Transfer tool when the Log and Capture tool is open produces the error message, "Alert Log and Transfer cannot be opened while Log and Capture is running. Please close Log and Capture and try again."

You can open the Log and Transfer tool by choosing File menu ⇨ Log and Transfer, or by using the Shift+⌘+8 key combination (see figure 3.9).

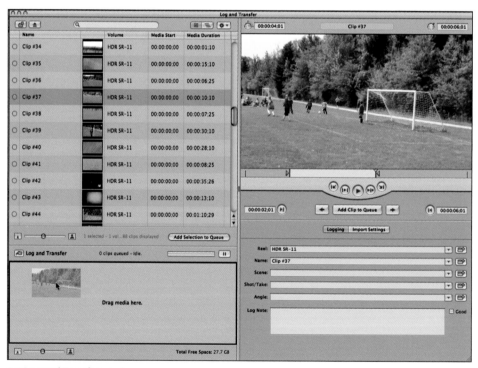

3.9 Log and Transfer window.

The Log and Capture tool has four main sections. These are the Browse, Preview, Logging, and Transfer Queue sections.

The Browse section provides the clip information shown in Table 3.2.

Table 3.2 Clips in Browser

Browse Section	Function
Clip name	Name of the volume.
Thumbnail	Displays the first frame of a clip; you cannot change the poser frame.
Volume	Name of the volume or disk that the image clip is on.
Media Start	Always 00:00:00:00 for AVCHD footage.
Media Duration	Length of the clip.

The Preview section provides functionality for previewing the footage, setting in and out points, and adding clips to the Transfer Queue. The Logging section allows you to add information such as scene, shot or take, angle, and additional log notes. The Transfer Queue lists the clips queued for ingest and their ingest status.

Ingesting media

Use the following steps to ingest your media:

1. **Connect your device using FireWire or USB.** The storage media appears as a mounted volume on the desktop.

2. **Check your scratch disk to make sure it has enough storage available for the amount of media you plan to record.**

3. **Select a logging bin where the clips will be saved in your project.**

4. **Open the Log and Transfer tool by choosing File menu ⇨ Log and Transfer, or pressing ⌘+Shift+8.** The Log and Transfer tool opens, detects the attached device, and opens the media files in the Browse section.

5. **Select a clip in the Browse section to open it in the Preview section.**

6. **View the footage and set the in and out points.**

7. **Add any information that you want to be logged with the clip in the Logging section.**

8. **Select the audio and video tracks to be ingested in the Import Settings pane in the Logging section.** Some formats allow grouping of pairs of audio channels as stereo or dual mono. Some formats automatically mix the audio down to stereo and cannot be adjusted in this pane.

9. **Click the Add Clip to Queue button in the Preview area to ingest the clip.** The clip appears in the Transfer Queue section. The clip's transfer status and a progress bar appear at the top of this section. As soon as a clip is added to the queue, ingestion begins. You can continue to review clips and add them to the queue while clips in the queue are being ingested. This process is much more efficient than logging clips and batch-capturing them after logging has been completed.

As clips are recorded into the system, status dots indicate which clips have been successfully ingested. Status dots that are half-filled indicate that only a specific section of the clip has been recorded. A full dot indicates the entire clip has been recorded.

Genius

It is not necessary to have the recording device itself connected to the computer. You can save data from file-based recording systems and open them as volumes on other or larger hard drives. Use the Add Folder button at the top-left corner of the Browse section of the Log and Transfer tool to open these volumes.

Caution

You should give the volume name on the transfer drive a descriptive name before logging clips in case you have to recapture them in the future.

Importing Media

There are various ways to import media into Final Cut Pro. After choosing File menu ⇨ Import, you can import individual clips or an entire folder.

When you import media, Final Cut Pro references its original location. Do not import media directly from a DVD or any other removable source that's not intended to stay with the system. Once that particular source has been removed, the referenced media becomes offline.

Caution

You can drag individual QuickTime files or folders directly from OS X into the Browser window; you do not need to use the Import menu. This is particularly useful if you have two monitors connected to your system. You can use the second monitor for using the OS X finder.

Genius

Importing files recorded in FCP format

Certain manufacturers, such as Focus Enhancements, make a line of hard disk recorders called Direct-to-Edit Recorders. Focus FS models allow clips to be recorded to removable FireWire disk drives in most popular native DV NLE file formats. You can connect the drives to a Mac computer through a FireWire cable. You can add media files from these disks to FCP by choosing File menu ➪ Import. These types of clips are available immediately for editing and do not have to be ingested.

Importing audio

You may bring audio into Final Cut Pro from a variety of sources. This includes files from an audio CD, MP3, WAV, or AIFF files. It's important to understand the various issues that arise when dealing with these different formats.

The most common audio sample-rate format for professional use is 48 kHz. Unfortunately, many consumer cameras are set to 32 kHz. Make sure you check the audio settings in your camera before shooting. Otherwise, 32 kHz may cause problems when it is imported into Final Cut Pro.

Caution

Audio sample-rate conversion

Audio from CDs has a sample rate of 44.1 kHz. Most DV projects and DVDs have an audio sample rate of 48 kHz. If you import audio directly from a CD, it is imported at 44.1 kHz and has to be converted before it is output to tape or DVD. It is better to convert the sample rate before you import the CD audio.

Converting with iTunes

Use the following steps to import and convert the CD audio files simultaneously:

1. **Choose iTunes ⇨ Preferences to open the iTunes preferences window.**

2. **Select the Advanced pane and select Importing.**

3. **Change the Import Using setting to AIFF Encoder.**

4. **Change the Setting from Automatic to Custom to open the AIFF Encoder window.**

5. **Set the Sample Rate to 48.000 kHz and the Sample Size to 16 bit; leave the Channels setting at Auto.**

Once you've followed these steps, you can right-click any music file within the iTunes music library and, from the contextual menu, choose Convert Selection to AIFF (see figure 3.10). This creates a new audio file based on your iTunes preferences.

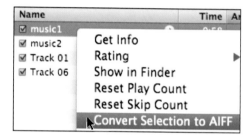

3.10 Converting the audio sample rate with iTunes.

Caution If you plan on using iTunes to perform audio sample-rate conversions, make note of the default iTunes storage location, which is Mac HD ⇨ users ⇨ *username* ⇨ Music ⇨ iTunes ⇨ iTunes Music. You may want to change this location to something else.

Converting audio with QuickTime Pro

You can also use QuickTime Pro to convert an audio clip to 48 kHz. This requires that you have the Pro version of QuickTime installed on your computer. Fortunately, as long as you have Final Cut Pro installed, Final Cut Pro automatically upgrades your version of QuickTime to QuickTime Pro.

Use the following steps to convert the CD audio files.

1. **Open the file in QuickTime Pro.**

2. **Choose File menu ⇨ Export to open the Export File window.**

3. **Choose AIFF from the Export drop-down menu.**

4. **Click the Options button to open the Sound Settings window.**

5. **Change the Rate to 48.000 and leave the Sample Size at 16.**

6. **Select the file location for the transcoded file.** This should be the same location as the other project files.

Working with MPEG files

Final Cut Pro has the ability to play all sorts of video formats directly within the timeline. However, some video formats may require a format conversion before they work correctly within Final Cut Pro.

MPEG is a common video file format that you may run across. MPEG-2 is used for standard DVDs and multimedia use. MPEG-1 is strictly used for multimedia use. Importing an MPEG file directly into Final Cut Pro only imports the video portion of the file. You do not hear any audio. This is because the MPEG file is muxed together. The term *muxed* means the audio and video streams are embedded together.

Because the video and audio are not separate streams, Final Cut Pro is unable to play the audio. You will encounter the exact same problem if you attempt to import files directly from a DVD. DVD files are in VOB format. VOB stands for video object, which is a container for the media within a DVD. VOB files are based on the MPEG-2 file type, which means you need to demux the file if you plan on using the audio from the DVD.

Fortunately, there is free software available that demuxes VOB or MPEG files. I recommend a software product called MPEG Streamclip, which is available at www.squared5.com. It's a must-have for those who need to convert MPEG files for use within Final Cut Pro.

Genius

If you are recording with a camera that records to mini-DVD, like a Sony Handycam, using iMovie8 offers a solution. iMovie8 reads the DVD and prompts the user to create an event. This creates a folder for the media and breaks the MPEG-2 file into self-contained QuickTime movies based on the start/stop metadata.

Managing Media

Nothing is more important than managing your media within Final Cut Pro. It is a critical mistake not to pay attention to media management.

Caution

When you rename clips within the Browser window, note that Final Cut Pro does not rename the files that those clips are pointing to.

Fortunately, there are two functions that allow you to reestablish the naming structure so that the clips in the Browser window match the names of the clips that they are referencing. You have two choices: Clip to Match File and File to Match File.

- **Clip to Match File.** This updates filenames within the Browser window to match the name of the mediafile on a hard drive.

- **File to Match File.** This updates the media filenames on the hard drive to match the names of clips within the Browser window. Because you'll be working with and organizing clips within the Browser window, this is a more common choice.

To update mediafiles on your hard drive to match the names of clips within Final Cut Pro, follow these steps:

1. **Select a group of clips within the Browser window.**

2. **Right-click on any of the selected clips' icons to reveal the contextual menu (see figure 3.11) and choose the Rename menu ⇨ File to Match Clip.** Mac OS X warns you that you are about to modify a source file. Click OK to continue.

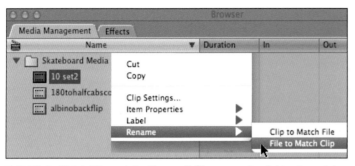

3.11 File to Match Clip updates the mediafile on your hard drive to match.

Storage Requirements

Storage requirements are often a mystery to people. How much storage does this stuff really take up? The answer to that can be somewhat complex because it depends on what media formats, or *codecs*, you are using (see Table 3.3).

Table 3.3 Format Storage Requirements

Video Format	Storage Requirements
DV	3.5MB/sec
HDV	3.2MB/sec *variable
HD	13.9MB/sec

If you do the math, 5 minutes of DV video takes up approximately 1GB of space! Another confusing factor is that HDV is generally considered to have three times better quality than DV. So if you look at the chart above, how in the world does HDV take up less space than DV? The trick is in the compression.

HDV works with a variable compression scheme, which means that every frame is compressed differently. HDV also works with MPEG-2 compression, which relies on intraframe and temporal compression. If your video frame contains a lot of details, the file size of HDV may average out to be higher than DV. In general, HDV usually takes up a smaller footprint than DV. I find this to be quite amazing considering the increased quality over DV.

When you get to full HD, you can see that the file size is much higher. Four times higher! Working in full HD often requires something called a *storage array*, in which a group of hard drives works together for the amount of bandwidth required to play back the media.

Which Editing
Technique Fits My Style?

There are many different ways to edit in Final Cut Pro, and it's important to discover which style is most efficient for the needs of your specific project. Editing a feature-length film is very different from editing a music video. In addition, all editors have their own style in terms of accomplishing each task. A lot of editors edit from the beginning of a sequence to the end of a sequence. While that may make sense, it may not be the best workflow in terms of editing efficiency. Remember that you are working with a non-linear editing system.

Editing Workflow

There are many different ways to edit in Final Cut Pro, but there are some critical features that should not be ignored. I'm going to assume that you are familiar with the basics of editing. This means that you're familiar with marking in and out points, and that you know the difference between an overwrite edit and an insert edit. I'll focus on some concepts and techniques that may not be apparent to even the most seasoned editor.

What if I told you that there was a way to edit an entire program without using any in or out points? Then what if I told you that you could edit an entire program without dragging or dropping any clips to the Timeline? Yes, that's right! It sounds crazy, but marking in points and out points, and dragging clips to a sequence can be very inefficient. I'm not asking you to change your editing style, but you should keep an open mind as you read forward.

Using the Add Edit feature

The Add Edit feature is one of the most valuable editing tools when it comes to working with Final Cut Pro. You can use the Add Edit feature to add markers to your sequence as you play along. These markers automatically turn into edit points. The idea here is to use the add-edit function to place edit points based on a voiceover track; then you can place clips into the spaces that you've created. This method provides for a true non-linear workflow.

To demonstrate this, assume you are putting together a 30-second promo or commercial. Here is a quick exercise on how a non-linear workflow functions.

1. **Edit the voiceover track onto A1.** Turn on the audio waveforms for the clips within the Timeline.

2. **Turn on the audio waveforms.** Within the Timeline layout menu (see figure 4.1), click the audio waveforms option. Using the audio waveform is a critical function when placing edit points. You can use the audio waveform to help you make edit decisions because it will be obvious where certain words of dialog appear.

3. **Generate some slug.** The term *slug* refers to a blank piece of media that is used for filler. You access slug from the Generators menu (see figure 4.2). Ideally, you want to make enough slug to match the amount of audio on A1.

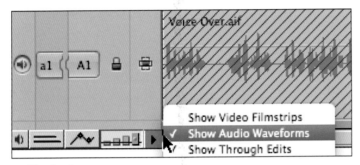

4.1 Timeline layout menu.

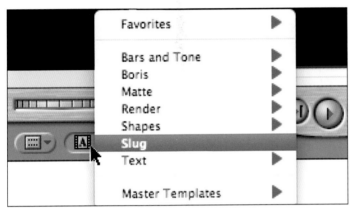

4.2 Slug from the Generators menu.

4. **Disconnect the audio track panels in your sequence.** This allows you to edit video-only slug to the Timeline. Also, it's a good idea to lock the A1 audio track to prevent changes to the audio (see figure 4.3).

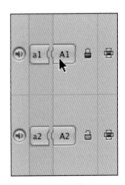

4.3 Disconnecting audio track destination patches.

5. **Add 30 seconds of slug to V1 directly over the voiceover clip that's on A1.** If the slug isn't long enough, trim out some additional slug to match the duration of the audio track below.

6. **Place edit points as you play through the sequence.** As you move the playhead indicator through the sequence, use the keyboard shortcut Ctrl+V to place edit marks at each line of dialog.

Alternatively, you can use the Blade tool to do the same thing. The one advantage of using the Add Edit feature is that you can mark points on the fly. In other words, you don't need to stop the playhead indicator in order to mark edit points. This is useful if you are trying to mark edit points based on the beat of a music track.

7. **Use the Replace Edit function to drop in clips based on the edit points that you've made.** The Replace Edit button is the blue button located in the lower-left corner of the Canvas window (see figure 4.4). You can also use the keyboard shortcut F11. The Replace Edit function automatically fills a clip based on the position of the yellow playhead indicators. It uses the position of the playhead indicator in the Viewer window as a starting point, and then fills in the media forward and backward based on the position of the playhead indicator in the Timeline.

By using this method of editing, you'll find a tremendous increase in your editing efficiency and speed. Adding the edit points ahead of time allows you to replace areas of the sequence that are obvious edit choices. Then, you can go back and work on the areas that require more thought. The important lesson here is that you do not need to edit your sequence in a linear way from beginning to end. Using the Add Edit feature allows you to pinpoint areas throughout the sequence that you can put together without having to tackle the beginning of the sequence.

Genius

You can map the Add Edit feature to a key on the keyboard. This way, you can press just a single key to perform the add-edit function, instead of having to press Ctrl+V. For more information about modifying the keyboard layout, see Chapter 2.

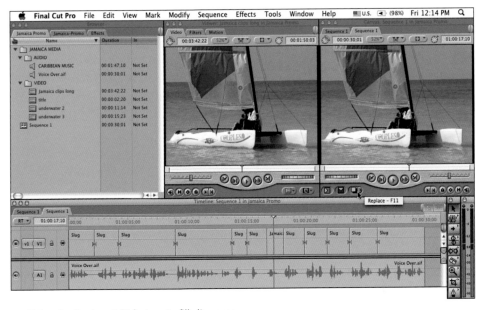

4.4 Using the Replace Edit feature to fill clip areas.

How to slip content

Using the add-edit and replace-edit methods is a fantastic way to get started when putting together a sequence. However, you'll definitely find spots in your sequence where the content doesn't quite start or end at the right point within the space provided. You can use a trimming function called *slip* to adjust a clip's in and out points without changing its position in the Timeline.

To slip a clip's contents, follow these steps:

1. **Double-click the clip that you want to adjust within the sequence.** This opens the clip in the Viewer window. Within the Viewer window, you see the in and out points of the clip you are adjusting. The bottom portion of the Viewer window shows small film sprockets to indicate that you are adjusting a clip within the Timeline window.

2. **Hold down the Shift key while dragging the in point of the clip within the Viewer window.** This shifts the in and out points of the clip without moving or changing the clip's duration in the Timeline window.

The snapping feature

Final Cut Pro is a visually oriented program. Therefore, most users are going to drag clips from either the Browser window or the Viewer window directly into the Timeline. This works fine for many types of jobs. When you drag and drop clips into a sequence, they may have a magnetic property, meaning that the clips automatically snap to other clips within the sequence. This magnetic property is called *snapping*. The N key toggles the snapping feature on and off. It is probably one of the most common shortcut keys that you'll use in Final Cut Pro.

I catch a lot of users clicking the Snapping icon in the upper-right corner of the Timeline window (see figure 4.5). It's a big waste of energy and efficiency to constantly be clicking up there. Learn to use the shortcut N key to toggle the snapping feature on and off.

4.5 Snapping icon in the Timeline window.

Overwrite vs. insert editing

The terms *overwrite* and *insert* refer to how clips are added to the Timeline. When you drag a clip to the Timeline window, one of two things happens: Either an overwrite edit or an insert edit is performed. Within each track of a sequence, there is an insert/overwrite divider line. This line determines whether an overwrite edit or an insert edit is performed.

For an overwrite edit, the clip is placed directly where you drop it off without affecting other surrounding clips (see figure 4.6). It also replaces whatever clip was underneath it. When dropping off a clip to perform an overwrite edit, make sure the cursor turns into a downward arrow by dropping off the clip below the insert/overwrite line.

4.6 Overwrite edit.

For an insert edit, the clip is placed directly where you drop it off, but all the clips underneath it and to the right of it are pushed over to the right (see figure 4.7). When dropping off a clip to perform an insert edit, make sure the cursor turns into a sideways arrow by dropping off the clip above the insert/overwrite line.

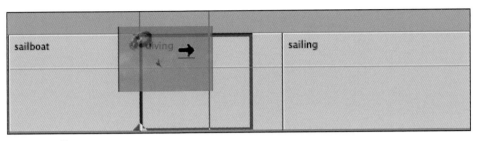

4.7 Insert edit.

Caution The Selection tool is the most commonly used tool in Final Cut Pro. It allows you to easily trim and move clips around within a sequence. When you activate other tools such as the Zoom tool, you should make it a common practice to go back to the Selection tool by pressing the A key.

Managing the Timeline

One of the most important skills of editing with Final Cut Pro is the ability to manage the Timeline window. Sequences can become incredibly complex and may contain thousands of edit points. It's important that you are able to manage your sequences efficiently.

Zoom slider bar

The Zoom slider bar at the bottom of the Timeline window is what allows you to zoom in and out of a sequence. Using the Zoom slider bar is a bit torturous on your hands; after a long editing session, you'll begin to understand why.

Zoom function

You can also use the Zoom tool within the tool palette to zoom in and out of a sequence. Click the Zoom icon or press the Z key to activate the Zoom tool. Each time you click within a sequence, the sequence zooms in closer to individual clips. To zoom out, hold down the option key while clicking a sequence.

Instead of using the Zoom slider bar, use the keyboard shortcuts ⌘++ and ⌘+– to zoom in and out of a sequence. Then use the Fit to Window command to fit the entire sequence inside the Timeline window. A good general workflow would be to quickly zoom into a section of the sequence that you want to work on, and then press Shift+Z to see the entire sequence.

Fit to Window

Fit to Window is a shortcut command that you'll use often. When you use the keyboard shortcut Shift+Z, Final Cut Pro automatically adjusts the contents of a sequence window to fit within the size of the window.

Moving clips around

You can move clips around within a sequence by using the Selection tool. The Selection tool is located at the top of the Final Cut Pro tool palette. Using the Selection tool is as easy as dragging clips to their proper locations. You can also trim the edges of a clip by grabbing the clip's edge and dragging it to the left or right.

Closing gaps

When moving content around, you are sometimes left with gaps within a sequence. You can close a gap by right-clicking in the gap area and selecting Close Gap from the contextual menu (see figure 4.8).

4.8 Closing gaps by right-clicking in the gap area.

Using the track forward and backward tools

When working with large sequences, it is sometimes necessary to insert additional material in the middle of a sequence. Occasionally, you may run into a situation where you need to make room for another scene. You can use the track forward or backward tools (see figure 4.9) to select all the clip's elements from a particular point to easily move them down to make room for the new content.

If you choose to select all tracks forward and you have long stretches of music or voiceover content, you may need to use the Blade tool to create artificial edit points prior to moving your content. Otherwise, your entire music bed and voiceover track moves without providing an area to add additional content.

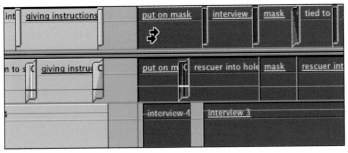

4.9 Moving clips using track forward tools.

Managing track heights

Final Cut Pro provides the ability to resize each track within a sequence. There are also track height presets that automatically resize the tracks for you. The toggle for the Timeline track height is located in the lower-left corner of the Timeline window. You can use the keyboard shortcut Shift+T to cycle through the various track sizes.

You can also manually adjust each track by placing the mouse cursor just below each track until the mouse cursor changes into the resize indicator. Drag the corresponding track to the size that you prefer.

Working with multiple sequences

When working on a large project, you should create separate sequences for each scene. You can then assemble all the scenes together into a larger sequence.

To edit several sequences together, follow these steps:

1. **Double-click each sequence within the Browser window.** This automatically opens each sequence as its own tab within the Timeline window.

2. **Tear off one of the sequence tabs within the Timeline window (see figure 4.10).** This creates another Timeline window containing the sequence that you've torn off.

3. **Drag the contents of one sequence to another sequence by highlighting clips in one of the Timeline windows and dragging it to the other Timeline window.**

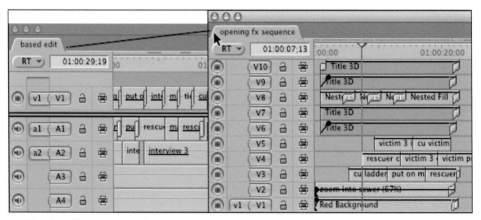

4.10 Tearing off a sequence tab.

I recommend that you perform this procedure last. Once you've combined multiple sequences into a larger sequence, it becomes difficult to manage any changes that you may need to make. It's best if you can keep everything segmented until it's absolutely necessary to assemble everything for final output.

Creating a Montage

A practical editing job is creating a montage of clips that transition from one clip to another. You'll sometimes hear the term *slideshow*, which basically refers to the same concept of having a bunch of video images or stills that transition from one clip to another with a music bed.

There are some excellent editing techniques that you can use to improve your workflow when building these types of sequences. Start with a folder of still images. By default, Final Cut Pro gives you 2 minutes of referenced time for each still image that you import. It also marks at an area of 10 seconds in the middle of each 2-minute clip. This is fantastic, because it means you'll have plenty of room for transitions between each image.

When you import images into Final Cut Pro, the system always uses the still/freeze duration setting within the user preferences for the distance between the in and out points (see figure 4.11). The default duration is 10 seconds. Changing this setting does not change the amount of referenced media, which is always 2 minutes. This setting only changes the distance between the in and out points.

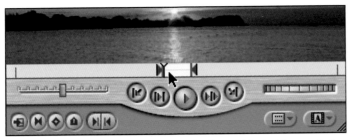

4.11 Still import duration preference marks clips within the Viewer window.

When importing elements into Final Cut Pro, you can simply drag a folder directly from the Finder into the Browser window. Final Cut Pro mirrors the directory structure and references the media from the location that you've dragged the files from. You can even drag a folder full of images from the Finder directly to the Timeline. Final Cut Pro automatically places all the images into a sequence. The duration of the clips is based on the still/freeze duration setting specified in the user preferences.

Caution
When importing clips from the Finder window, keep in mind that Final Cut Pro refer-ences the media from whatever location you drag the clips from. Therefore, do not drag elements from removable forms of media such as a DVD or thumb-drive. When those devices are removed, Final Cut Pro can no longer find the media.

After a sequence has been created with all the still images, you can easily change the duration of all the clips without having to reimport them.

1. **Highlight all the clips within the sequence by using the keyboard shortcut ⌘+A.**

2. **Right-click one of the highlighted clips.** Choose Duration from the contextual menu.

3. **Type in a new duration.** All the clips automatically conform to the new duration.

Rearranging clips using the swap edit function

Another powerful feature is the ability to rearrange your clips once they've been added to a sequence. You can use the swap edit function to rearrange your clips. The official Final Cut Pro ter-minology for the term *swap* is a bit misleading, because this function allows you to rearrange clips instead of actually swapping one clip for another.

To rearrange your clips using the swap function, follow these steps:

1. **Highlight a clip that you want to move within your sequence.**

2. **Turn on the snapping function.**

3. **Drag the clip to its new location while you continue to hold down the mouse button.**

4. **Hold down the option key and release the mouse button.** Look for the Swap Edit tool before you release the mouse button. Holding down the option key turns the Selection tool into the Swap Edit tool (see figure 4.12).

Caution
When rearranging clips, you may need to practice these steps a few times to become familiar with the exact procedure. If you hold down the option key too soon, Final Cut Pro copies your clip instead of rearranging the clips. The trick is to move the clip to its new location first and then hold down the option key.

4.12 Using the swap edit function.

Applying multiple transitions between all your clips

You can apply transitions to clips by right-clicking between any edit point and choosing Add Transition from the contextual menu. The transition within the contextual menu refers to the default transition within the effects palette.

You can change the default transition by following these steps:

1. **Click the Effects tab within the Browser window.**

2. **Click the disclosure triangle to expand the video transitions category.** Find an appropriate transition effect that you would like to use between your clips.

3. **Right-click a transition and choose Set Default Transition from the contextual menu (see figure 4.13).** The transition appears with an underline. The underline represents the fact that the transition is now set as the default.

You can also apply the default transition by using the keyboard shortcut ⌘+T. A good strategy for adding multiple transitions fairly quickly is to advance to each edit point and then press ⌘+T to add the default transition.

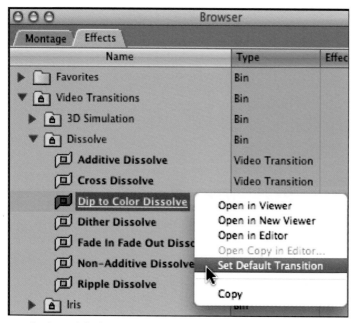

4.13 Setting a default transition.

You can use the up and down arrows on the keyboard to quickly advance to an edit point within a sequence. The workflow would be as follows:

1. **Press the down arrow on the keyboard.** This automatically advances the playhead indicator to the next edit point.

2. **Use the keyboard shortcut ⌘+T to add the default transition.**

3. **Repeat steps 1 and 2 until you've added all the necessary transitions.**

You can also add multiple transitions to all the clips at the same time by highlighting all the clips within a sequence and dragging them up into the Canvas window into the Overwrite with Transition box (see figure 4.14). Make sure the playhead indicator is parked at the first frame of the highlighted clips, because you're overwriting the clips on top of themselves.

4.14 Overwrite with transition.

If you add hundreds of transitions and then decide later that you do not want them, you would normally have to remove each transition independently. You can remove all the transitions by highlighting your sequence, dragging all the clips into the Canvas window, and dropping them off into the Overwrite box. This overwrites the entire sequence on top of itself, and removes all the transitions. Again, make sure the playhead indicator is parked at the first frame of the highlighted clips within your sequence before you drag the clips up into the Canvas window.

Trimming with the Option Key

By default, Final Cut Pro likes to keep clip elements in synch. This means that if you record a clip that contains audio and video content, the audio and video elements stay together. If a clip's name is underlined within a sequence, this means that its audio and video contents are linked together.

In the upper-right corner of the Timeline menu, you see a linking icon. When the linking icon is turned on, this tells Final Cut Pro to keep clips that contain audio and video content linked together.

Caution

I recommend that you always keep the linking icon turned on. Otherwise, you risk having synch issues if you forget to turn the linking icon back on.

Fortunately, you can use the option key to temporarily break the linking relationship between linked audio and video content. This allows you to quickly delete or trim audio or video without having to constantly worry about whether or not the linked selection icon is turned on. The option key works with the Selection tool, the Blade tool, or any of the trim tools.

For example, if you wanted to delete just the audio portion of a linked clip, hold down the option key and click the audio portion of the clip. Then press the Delete key to remove just the audio.

Caution

There are two different Delete keys on a standard Apple keyboard. The large Delete key lifts out a clip, leaving a gap. The small Delete key performs a ripple delete, which removes the clip contents and closes the gap.

How Do I Use Final Cut Pro as a Professional Sound and Mixing Tool?

Final Cut Pro includes several audio tools for audio mixing on a professional level. Furthermore, it is integrated with Soundtrack Pro, which is a full-fledged audio editor and sound design program. It's up to you to determine the best workflow for the type of job that you are working on.

Mixing Audio Levels

There are a variety of different workflows when it comes to mixing audio levels within Final Cut Pro.

For example, you can edit projects by cutting video with its corresponding audio into a sequence, and add music and sound effects later. This is most commonly done with larger projects, such as scripted film, television programs, and documentaries. For shorter projects such as news and television commercials, you may want to start with a basic narrative soundtrack and add video to it, adding music and sound effects later. Or, you can use a combination of these two methods. Think of long-format projects that contain sections of video cut to voiceovers, such as the movie *Fight Club*.

Regardless of how a sequence is created, additional audio tracks containing music, sound effects, and voiceovers are often added to it. The audio levels of the individual tracks need to be adjusted so that the proper message is conveyed. As an example, if you are putting music into a scene, the voiceover track should be at least six decibels louder than the music for the words to be heard. All of the audio tracks are combined to produce the final audio output.

After the relative levels of the individual clips have been adjusted, the overall volume of the sequence needs to be adjusted. To demonstrate this, I'll start by building a sequence with 10 seconds of bars and tone created by the Generator menu (see figure 5.1). This automatically loads 2 minutes of bars and tone into the Viewer window. Final Cut Pro automatically marks an area of 10 seconds in the middle of the clip.

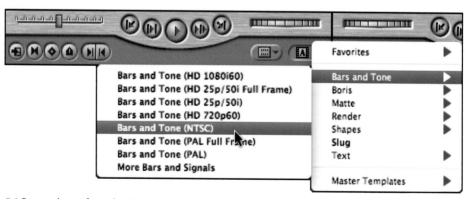

5.1 Bars and tone from the Generator menu.

If you place the bars and tone into the timeline, notice that the audio volume is -12dB in both the left and right channels, as shown by the audio meter during playback. If you were to add two more audio tracks and overwrite the audio from the bars and tone into these tracks, the audio volume would be -6dB in both the left and right channels (see figure 5.2).

5.2 Audio meter at -6dB.

The process of combining audio tracks into channels is called *mixing*. As you can see, adding audio tracks increases the overall volume without changing the volume of any of the individual tracks or clips. For television programs, the desired maximum volume is -6dB.

To adjust clips in a sequence, you can use the Audio Mixer tool. You can open the Audio Mixer tool from the Tools menu (Tools ⇨ Audio Mixer) or by using the keyboard combination Option+6. The Audio Mixer tool is designed to look like a hardware audio mixer with controls for each track that contains audio, as well as a master control (see figure 5.3). The volume and panning for an individual clip is adjusted using the track controls.

Audio downmix

Audio Mute

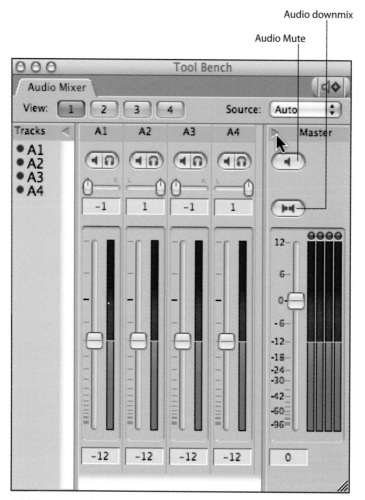

5.3 Master control slider with Audio Downmix and Audio Mute buttons.

Adjusting the Levels in the Timeline

There are a variety of ways that you can adjust audio levels. For example, you can mix audio levels directly within the Final Cut Pro Timeline. This can be accomplished with either the audio mixer or a process that uses something called an audio rubber band.

Master Control Slider

There is a hidden master control slider within the Audio Mixer tool. The master control slider affects the output volume of the entire sequence. It's the very last thing you would adjust when you are ready to output. You need to click the right-facing triangle in the upper-right corner of the Audio Mixer window to reveal the master audio control slider. If you have a sequence that is set to output independent audio tracks, the master control slider is the only tool that displays the audio level for each individual track.

You can toggle between a downmix and individual track levels by clicking the Audio Downmix button. Pressing the Audio Downmix button causes all individual tracks to output as a stereo pair. For more information on configuring a sequence with multiple audio outputs, see Chapter 2.

Using the audio mixer

The Audio Mixer window uses individual sliders that adjust the audio levels for each individual clip within a sequence (see figure 5.4). It provides audio sliders for each clip within a sequence for where the playback indicator is parked. For example, if the playback indicator is parked over four audio clips, the Audio Mixer provides four audio sliders.

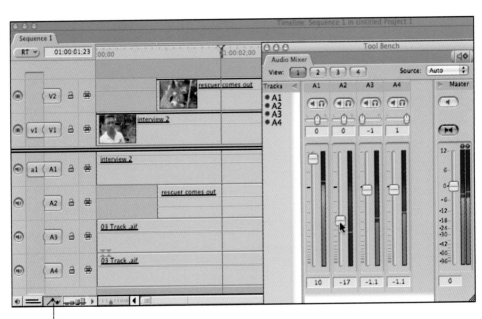

Toggle clip overlays

5.4 Using the Audio Mixer tool to adjust individual clips within a sequence.

Clips that have green triangles within them represent stereo clips. Their audio levels automatically move together.

The goal here is to have the voiceover be approximately 6dB over the ambient at all times, with a peak volume level for the sequence at -6dB. That's why you'll notice that the slider for the voiceover track is pushed up quite high. You will also notice some pink lines within each audio clip. These pink lines are called audio clip overlays. They represent an audio level adjustment from a clip's original audio level.

If you need to have various audio levels within a single clip that is in a sequence, you can use the Blade tool to break the clip in half (see figure 5.5). Because the clip is now in two pieces, you can have two different audio levels.

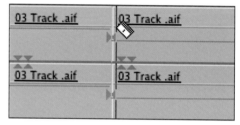

5.5 Using the Blade tool to cut audio clips into two pieces for audio adjustments.

Genius

After using the Blade tool to cut a clip into two pieces, you can use an audio transition or cross fade to smooth out the audio level adjustments. You can do this by right-clicking the transition point and selecting Add Transition 'Cross Fade' from the contextual menu within the sequence.

Using the Pen tool

You can use the Pen tool in the timeline when clip overlays are turned on to create and modify keyframes. Keyframes allow you to modify volume values at any point in a clip. The values are interpolated between keyframes.

To adjust the audio levels of clips using keyframes, follow these steps:

1. **Activate the clips overlays feature.** This displays the pink clip overlay lines within all the clips in your sequence.

2. **Activate the Pen tool by pressing the P key.** This turns the Selection tool into a Pen tool.

3. **Use the Pen tool to add a series of keyframes within the confines of a clip (see figure 5.6).** To add a keyframe, position the cursor over the audio level line until it changes from an arrow to a pen icon.

4. **Click the mouse button to add individual keyframes.**

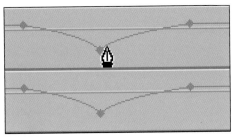

5.6 Using the Pen tool to add audio keyframes.

Keyframes are illustrated by pink diamonds that are placed on the audio level line. For linked stereo tracks, keyframes are placed at the same time on both tracks.

You can change keyframe audio levels by placing the cursor over the keyframe and dragging it up to increase volume, or down to decrease volume. You can use the same process to move keyframes horizontally, changing their position in time. A text box opens, displaying volume and timeline position changes as you move the keyframe.

Caution It is good practice to press the A key to reactivate the Selection tool after you are done with the Pen tool. Most of the functions within Final Cut Pro are performed with the Selection tool.

Adjusting the levels of multiple clips

It's sometimes necessary to adjust the levels of multiple clips at the same time. You can do this by highlighting a group of clips with the Selection tool, and using the keyboard shortcuts Ctrl++ or Ctrl+- to increase or decrease the audio levels of all the selected clips. You can also accomplish the same task by selecting Modify ➪ Audio ➪ Gain. I find it much easier to use the keyboard equivalents than the menu.

Adjusting audio in the viewer

You can adjust both the volume and panning in the viewer. First, double-click a clip to open it in the viewer. Instead of adding keyframes directly in the timeline, you can add them in the Viewer window. In addition, any keyframes that have been previously set in the timeline are displayed.

You can change panning and volume using the Panning and Level sliders. If the timeline indicator is not positioned on a keyframe, changing the panning or level creates a keyframe at the location where the value is changed.

In the example shown in figure 5.7, you could create an effect where the audio moves from the left speaker to the right speaker to create the illusion of the car racing past the listener. The area highlighted in dark gray is one frame wide. You can have up to 100 keyframes in this region. However, you need to zoom in relatively close in order to place more than a couple of keyframes within the highlighted area.

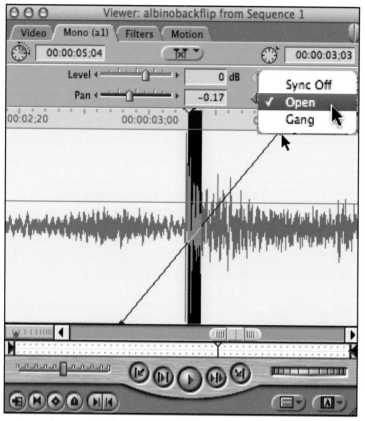

5.7 Adjusting audio levels and pan in the Viewer window.

Adjusting audio levels in the Viewer window offers the advantage of being able to see a larger waveform. To assist you in adjusting audio levels, I recommend that you set the playhead synch menu to Open within the Viewer window (see figure 5.7). When you set the playhead synch to On, the playhead indicator within the Viewer window synchronizes up to the playhead indicator in the Timeline window. Otherwise, it may be difficult to pinpoint specific areas within the Viewer window because its playhead indicator would be out of synch with the playhead indicator in the Timeline.

Using audio filters

Final Cut Pro has a set of audio filters located within the Effects tab. You can apply audio filters by dragging a particular filter to a clip within the Timeline window. You can stack an unlimited number of filters onto clips. Filters are processed in the order that they are applied.

In order to adjust and see the controls for each filter, you must double-click a particular audio clip to load its contents into the Viewer window. Click the Filters tab at the top of the window to reveal a list of audio filters that have been applied. Depending on your screen resolution, you may need to increase the size of the Viewer window in order to see the keyframe area for the audio controls.

Adding volume

A simple yet practical filter is the Gain filter, which provides you with additional volume control. Occasionally you will run into a problem where you are unable to increase the level of a clip high enough using the traditional audio mixer or audio clip overlays. Just drop an audio gain filter onto the clip, and you'll have the additional volume control you need.

Compressor/Limiter filter

If you are running short on time and you have a voiceover track where the audio is inconsistent, what do you do? Well, fortunately, there is a quick fix that may help you compress the audio levels so that you do not need to spot-check every single edit. It's the Compressor/Limiter filter. To use this filter, follow these steps:

1. **Navigate to the effects tab within the Final Cut Pro Browser window.** Find the Audio Filters/Final Cut Pro category.

2. **Drag the Compressor/Limiter filter to the clip(s) in your sequence.** It's best if you can apply the Compressor/Limiter filter to an entire track. Otherwise, you need to copy and paste the attributes to all the other clips to keep the compressor/limiter settings the same for your entire sequence.

3. **Double-click your clip to load it back into the Final Cut Pro Viewer window.** You should then see an audio Filters tab.

4. **Click the tab to adjust the settings (see figure 5.8).** Table 5.1 describes the available adjustments.

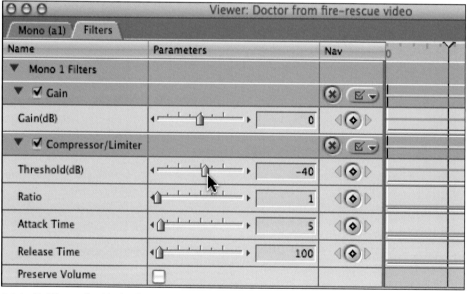

5.8 Audio Filters tab with the Compressor/Limiter filter.

The values for Attack and Release are generally fine. If you are using a relatively new version of Final Cut Pro, you can adjust these sliders in real time to hear changes. I typically use the scroll wheel on my mouse to adjust the sliders left or right while having my sequence set to play-loop so that I can adjust the parameters until I am happy.

Table 5.1 Compressor/Limiter Adjustments

Adjustment	Definition
Threshold slider	Defines how loud the loudest portion of the clip can be before compression is applied.
Ratio slider	Affects how much compression is applied. Be careful not to set this parameter too high.
Attack Time slider	Defines how long it takes for the filter to react to changes in volume.
Release Time slider	Defines how long it takes for the filter to react to how slowly the filter lets go of changes.

Using the Voice Over tool

The Voice Over tool is a great way to create a scratch track so that you can begin editing right away. There's no need to get hung up because you are waiting on the professional voiceover before you begin editing.

The Voice Over tool is located at Tools ⇨ Voice Over. Using the tool is quite simple; pressing the red button begins the recording process, and Final Cut Pro automatically records to a new track (see figure 5.9).

Caution In most cases, make sure you set the sample rate to 48,000Hz. To avoid audio feedback, plan on using some headphones, or as an alternative, make sure the output volume is turned all the way down while recording.

Genius Professional USB microphones allow you to use the Voice Over tool to create a professional voiceover track. A company called M-Audio makes an excellent device called an MBOX that provides professional-style XLR audio inputs. The box connects to your computer through a USB cable. By using a device like this, all you need is a professional microphone that runs into a soundproof room, and you now have the ability to produce professional voiceover audio.

5.9 The Voice Over tool.

Understanding Soundtrack Pro

Soundtrack Pro is a full digital audio workstation and more. It is tightly integrated with Final Cut Pro and provides an array of amazing music loops, sound effects, and audio filters. Soundtrack Pro certainly deserves an entire book to itself, but it's important to master some of the basic fundamentals in terms of how it works directly with Final Cut Pro.

Using Soundtrack Pro to build music and sound effects

You can send an entire sequence directly into Soundtrack Pro by using the Send To function in the File menu.

1. **Select a sequence in the Browser window.**

2. **Click File ⇨ Send To ⇨ Soundtrack Pro Multitrack Project.** A Save dialog appears. The default name is the sequence name with "(sent)" appended. This is so you do not save over the original media file.

You can also right-click a sequence directly within the Browser window and choose Send To ⇨ Soundtrack Pro Multitrack Project from the contextual menu. Final Cut Pro automatically creates a QuickTime reference file and sends it over to Soundtrack Pro with all the original audio tracks (see figure 5.10). Any audio level adjustments made in Final Cut Pro are also carried over into Soundtrack Pro, including any audio rubber bands that you have created.

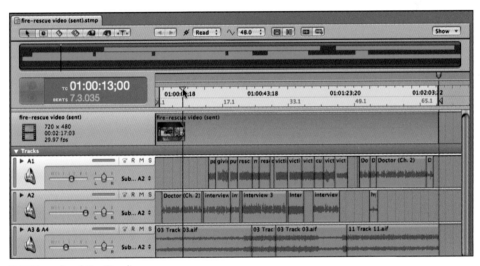

5.10 Soundtrack Pro Timeline.

Adding sound effects and scoring music

Final Cut Studio comes with a three-DVD music and sound effect library that contains thousands of music loops, longer compositions, and sound effects. You can access these sound files through the Search tab in the right pane. This tab has three main sections when seen with the keywords/matches view:

- **The upper-left section:** Displays keyword categories for the selection from the drop-down menu. You can subdivide keywords into topics including Sound Effects, Instruments, and Genres.

- **The upper-right section:** Labeled Matches, this section divides the items selected by keyword into style categories, such as Country/Folk and Dark.

- **The lower section:** Lists the files for the style category selected in the upper-right pane. It also lists the number of channels and tempo for each file and indicates if the media is online or offline by color; online files are listed in black, while offline files are listed in red.

Within the Search tab (see figure 5.11), you find different categories of sounds, including sound effects, instruments, and music loops. These sounds are tagged with keywords to make them easy to find. You can add sounds to the Soundtrack Pro Timeline by dragging them directly from the Search tab into the Timeline.

Installing additional music or sounds

You can obtain additional music and sound effects from Apple and third-party vendors. You can purchase Apple Jam Packs from the Apple Store. To install additional audio files on a system or network hard drive, follow these steps:

1. **Click the Setup button in the upper-right corner of the Search tab.** A setup window drops down from the Soundtrack Pro title bar.

2. **Click the + button in the upper-left corner of the setup window.** A Finder window opens.

3. **Navigate in the Finder window to the location where the audio files were installed and click the Open button.**

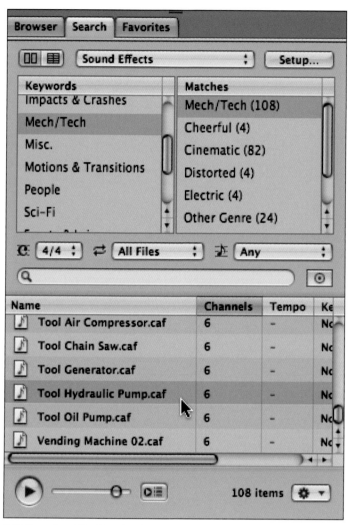

5.11 Soundtrack Pro Search tab.

Adjusting audio levels in Soundtrack Pro

You can adjust sound levels and audio pan directly within Soundtrack Pro (see figure 5.12). Setting points using envelopes is the Soundtrack Pro equivalent of setting audio keyframes in Final Cut Pro. Click the right-facing disclosure triangle to reveal the audio envelopes. You can add keyframes by double-clicking the audio or pan level line. To delete a keyframe, highlight it and press the Delete key.

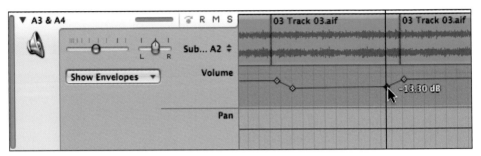

5.12 Adjusting volume/pan envelopes.

After you have finished adjusting, adding filters, sound effects, and a musical score, you can export the sequence so that it will be automatically imported back into your Final Cut Pro sequence.

To send the changes that you've made in Soundtrack Pro back to Final Cut Pro, follow these steps:

1. **Click File ⇨ Export.**

2. **Enter a filename and location for the exported file.** I recommend that you put the file in a folder within the folder that your Final Cut studio project is in. I always create a subfolder called Music and Sounds within my project folder to hold these files.

3. **Change the menu at the bottom of the dialog to After Export: Send Files to Final Cut Pro Sequence.** Leave all the other settings at their default values.

4. **Click Export.**

Observe the Import XML dialog in Final Cut Pro. Choose the sequence from the Destination drop-down menu; otherwise, a new Final Cut Pro project will be created. Final Cut Pro must remain open in the background in order for this process to work.

The sequence now has the mixdown audio tracks at the top. All of the original audio tracks are still included in the sequence, but they are muted. By keeping them in the sequence, they are available to be sent to Soundtrack Pro again, if necessary.

Using Soundtrack Pro filters

Soundtrack Pro also has a large set of audio filters. Although you can apply filters while in the multi-track editor, I find it most practical to apply audio filters using the Audio File editor. You can launch the Audio File editor by double-clicking a clip segment within the Soundtrack Pro Timeline.

Alternatively, you can send a file directly from a Final Cut Pro sequence into the Audio File editor (see figure 5.13) by right-clicking a clip and choosing Send To ⇨ Soundtrack Pro Audio File Project. Soundtrack Pro asks you to save the file with the word "sent" added to its name.

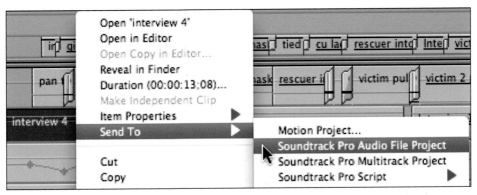

5.13 Sending an audio file from a Final Cut Pro sequence to the Soundtrack Pro Audio File editor.

You can add audio filters by using the Effects tab (see figure 5.14). Double-clicking an effect adds that particular filter to the sound file. There is no limit to the number of audio filters that you can apply to a clip.

Certain effects may have an Advanced button, which activates a separate control interface.

Removing noise

Removing noise is an interactive process. If the frequency of the noise is distinct and different from the frequency of the sound you want to retain, it is fairly easy to remove. If the noise is at the same frequency as the sound you want to retain, it may not be possible to remove it. Contrary to intuition, it is usually not good to remove 100 percent of the noise, as it can leave the audio sounding tinny.

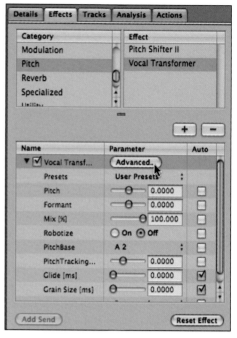

Use the following steps to reduce noise:

1. **Within the Audio File editor, highlight an area of the waveform that contains a specific noise print.** Preferably, this is an area where there is no human dialog.

5.14 Applying Soundtrack Pro audio filters.

2. **Drag the Selection tool in the timeline to mark an area to provide the noise sample.** To help you along, use the keyboard shortcuts ⌘++ or ⌘+- to zoom in or out of the waveform area. Use ⌘+Shift++ or ⌘+Shift+- to increase or decrease the waveform height.

3. **Click Process ⇨ Noise Reduction ⇨ Set Noise Print.** This stores the selection in a buffer.

4. **Highlight an area of the audio clip that you want to remove the noise from (see figure 5.15).** In some cases, this may be the entire clip. If this is the case, use the keyboard shortcut ⌘+A to select the entire clip.

5. **Click Process ⇨ Noise Reduction ⇨ Reduce Noise.** This activates the Reduce Noise dialog (see figure 5.16).

6. **Press the Play button in the bottom-left corner of the dialog and adjust the Noise Threshold until the selected noise disappears from the selected area.**

7. **Click File ⇨ Save.** Saving the changes also updates the Final Cut Pro sequence.

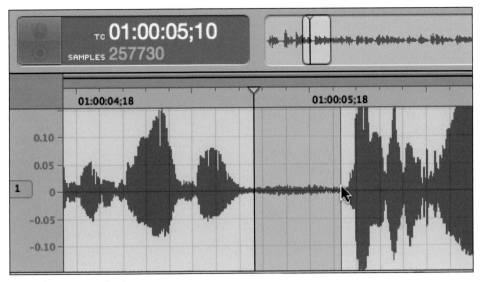

5.15 Select an area of noise.

5.16 The Reduce Noise dialog.

Using the frequency spectrum view

You can use the frequency spectrum view to remove areas of noise without completely removing an entire portion of the audio data. The secret is to click the Display Frequency Spectrum View button in the upper-right corner of the Soundtrack Pro interface.

To remove noisy areas of the audio spectrum, hold down the Option key while highlighting a specific area (see figure 5.17). Then press the Delete key. This removes only the highlighted area of the spectrum.

Normalization

Another common process is to normalize a clip or sequence. Normalization adjusts the peak volume of a clip to a specified level. For television broadcast, you want to set the Normalization Level to -6dB.

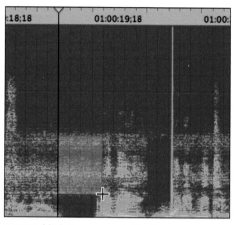

5.17 Highlighting an area in the frequency spectrum view.

1. **Select an area of the clip that you want to normalize.** In most cases, this will this be the entire clip audio file.

2. **Click Process ⇨ Normalize.** A parameter box appears.

3. **Set the Normalization level by adjusting the slider.** Then click OK.

Detecting common problems

You can analyze audio files for typical sound problems like clicks, pops, and ground hum, and remove them either all at once or on a case-by-case basis.

1. **Click the Analysis tab (see figure 5.18).**

2. **Select the check box for each condition you want to analyze.**

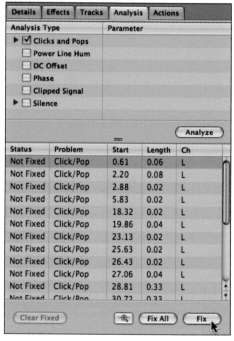

5.18 The Analysis tab.

3. **Click the Analyze button.** A status bar appears, showing you the progress of the analysis.

4. **Click the Fix or Fix All button to remove the problems.** The problem areas are marked in orange on the waveform and are listed at the bottom of the window (see figure 5.19).

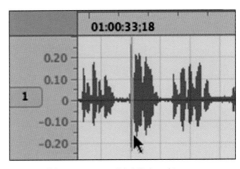

5.19 Problem areas are highlighted in orange.

There are ten different ways to create a title with Final Cut Pro. If you count LiveType and Motion, that brings the total to 12. Also, you can always use Adobe Photoshop or any other program that supports an alpha channel to create a title for Final Cut Pro. To help you narrow down your choices, you can perform most tasks by using either LiveType or Boris Title 3D. For example, if you are editing a car commercial, it may make sense to build all your titles using LiveType. If you need titles that have a 3D look to them, you can use Boris Title 3D.

Understanding Alpha Channels

In a very basic sense, an alpha channel represents a transparent area of an image. Imagine if you were able to design a logo on a piece of transparent glass. The glass would allow you to see what's underneath it. It's the same idea behind building a graphic with an alpha channel. The alpha channel allows non-linear editing systems to properly key graphic elements that contain transparency. In a typical scenario, these graphic elements are placed on a Video 2 track, which allows the graphic to be keyed over top of a Video 1 track.

An alpha channel isn't visible. Most software programs use a checkerboard pattern of gray and white squares to represent the transparent area (see figure 6.1). You also need to make sure that you save your final image as a file type that supports an embedded alpha channel. Bottom line, as long as you build your image or graphic on a transparent background, you are good to go.

6.1 The checkerboard pattern in the Canvas window shows the transparent area.

If an image format does not support an embedded alpha channel, you must create it manually. If possible, this is a step you want to avoid. It's much easier to use a format such as PNG or TIFF that automatically embeds the transparent area for you. Table 6.1 details some commonly used graphic formats.

Table 6.1 Commonly Used Graphic Formats

Graphic Format	Alpha Channel	Embedded Alpha	Layer Support
JPG	no	no	no
PNG	yes	yes	no
TGA	yes	no	no
PSD	yes	yes	yes
TIFF	yes	yes	yes
PICT	yes	no	no

Introducing LiveType

LiveType is bundled as part of Final Cut Studio. Don't bother looking for a hard-copy manual because it doesn't ship with one. However, you can access the documentation by choosing Help menu ⇨ LiveType User Manual. Technically, LiveType is an independent application. However, there is integration within Final Cut Pro that allows you to make changes to existing titles without having to redo your work.

At first glance, LiveType appears to have a very clean and slick interface that is easy to use. However, it's the power underneath the interface that makes LiveType so appealing. The interface is divided into four main quadrants, which are the Canvas, Inspector, Media Browser, and Timeline.

The software is relatively easy to use when creating titles that contain dynamic motion. In addition to animated effects, there are some amazing animated textures and objects that you can use to enhance the look of your titles.

Caution It's tempting to use LiveType for all of your titles. Be careful of falling into this trap, especially if you have hundreds of titles that you need to create. Even with the fastest MacBook Pro, the rendering time can test your patience if you have a bunch of complicated titles. Instead, consider using Boris Title 3D if you have many titles that you need to generate.

An easy way to learn LiveType is to open the various templates and manually deconstruct each effect (see figure 6.2). Templates generally consist of several track layers that can easily be changed by clicking a track layer and retyping the information within the text area of the Inspector window. LiveType includes a variety of templates that you can access by choosing File menu ⇨ Open Template.

6.2 Project templates include generic names within timeline tracks that you can change.

Background Properties

The default background setting within LiveType uses a transparent background. Zero-percent opacity represents a transparent background, which may seem a bit backward, but that's how it works. If for some reason you want to render the background so it is not transparent, you need to change the transparency to 100 percent and check the Render Background check box.

LiveType preferences

When you launch LiveType for the first time, make sure the project properties are set correctly to match your Final Cut Pro Sequence Settings. You can find the project properties by choosing Edit menu ⇨ Project Properties. For most U.S. consumers, you'll work with either NSTC DV 3:2 or HDV 1080i60. For most European consumers, you'll work with either CCIR 601 PAL, or HDV 1080i50. Regardless, the important step here is to make sure these settings match your Final Cut Pro sequence settings. Keep the field dominance set to none.

Caution It is critical that you tell LiveType to remember the current settings. Otherwise, when you relaunch LiveType, the project settings will reset back to the default settings. To save your settings, choose LiveType menu ⇨ Settings ⇨ Remember Settings.

Working with backgrounds and textures

LiveType contains a Media Browser window that contains all the LiveType media elements that you can use to build composites. There are a variety of textures and objects that are available to you. Keep in mind that these same textures and objects are also available to everyone else; there's nothing worse than presenting a video with canned effects for a high-end client.

The built-in textures and objects in LiveType are looping animations. You can either build or install additional textures and objects to enhance your videos. You can purchase additional backgrounds from various companies. Two companies that come to mind are www.LiveTypeCentral.com and www.digitaljuice.com. Within the Media Browser window, clicking the Textures tab reveals the various textures organized into categories. Some of the more interesting textures are located within the Digital and Space categories. You can add a texture to the LiveType timeline by double-clicking the texture. Textures appear as a blue-colored track within the timeline. It is important to keep in mind that textures are looping animations.

Notice that the timeline includes an in point and an out point (see figure 6.3). These points represent the area of the timeline that will be exported when you are finished. You want to adjust the in and out points accordingly.

In point

Out point

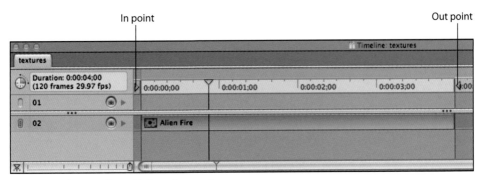

6.3 The Timeline window with in and out points.

 Caution   It is tempting to extend a texture by dragging out its contents within the LiveType timeline if you need more time. However, this slows down the animation speed of the actual texture.

You can easily change the hue, or color, of a texture by clicking the Attributes tab within the Inspector window and adjusting the Hue slider (see figure 6.4).

It is often necessary to extend the amount of time needed when working with a texture without slowing it down. Because all textures are designed as looping animations, you can extend the time by increasing the number of loops.

Follow these steps to extend the amount of time that media appears by specifying the number of loops:

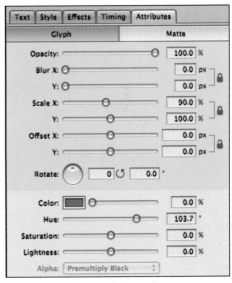

6.4 Adjusting the Hue slider to change texture color.

1. **Add a texture to an empty timeline by selecting a texture from the Media Browser and press the Apply to New Track button.**

2. **Click the Timing tab within the Inspector window.**

3. **Drag the Loop slider to the desired number of loops.**

Genius

You should make a habit of saving your work. To do so, choose File menu ⇨ Save as, and save your LiveType project. It's also a good habit to save all of your LiveType projects in a common place that is organized.

Importing looping backgrounds

A looping texture is a QuickTime movie where the first and last frames are the same. Companies like DigitalJuice provide thousands of looping animations that you can purchase. The process for importing textures, objects, and LiveFonts into the Media Browser is essentially the same. You can find these elements in the Mac HD ⇨ Library ⇨ Application Support ⇨ LiveType folder. It's not quite as simple as placing your background animations into the directory. The required elements are wrapped within an .lttx file extension.

You must use a special software module called FontMaker to create this file type. You can access this module by choosing File menu ⇨ FontMaker. Even though the module is labeled as FontMaker, it's required to create any textures, objects, or LiveFonts that appear within the Media Browser window.

FontMaker uses a script to automate the process of importing a texture into the LiveType Media Browser. You need to find your original Final Cut Studio install disc. Look for a folder called LiveType Extras. Copy the entire folder to your desktop. Open the Fontmaker Samples ⇨ Texture Sample folder. Inside, you'll see a sample texture, with a sample script.

The process is simple. You need to perform three steps:

1. **Create or purchase your looping animation.**

2. **Create a smaller preview version of the same movie.** Save it as an MP4 file.

3. **Change specific areas of the sample script to reflect the name of your animation.**

You can use QuickTime Pro to create the preview version of your file. Within QuickTime Pro, choose File menu ⇨ Export. Under the export submenu, choose Movie to MPEG-4.

The following code is the sample script you use to create a new file type. Remember to change the bold areas of the script to reflect the name of the new texture and preview file that you want to import into the Media Browser. It's only necessary to change the area in bold, as shown below. Leave everything else the same.

Texture Script

```
fontname "Texture"
dataname "Texture.afd"
proxyname "Texture.afp"
proxymovie "Texture Preview.mp4"
dvdname "My Disk Name"
cdname "My Disk Name"
flavor Texture
desc "My Description Here"
lowerleft 0 0
center 360 243
spacewidth 243
monowidth 720
fontsize 486
canloop 1
introframes 0
loopframes 45
endframes 0
rgbQuality 0.7
alphaQuality 0.7
framerate 30

-- Default Values

defaultsize 80
defaultjustify center
defaultspeed 100
defaultoutline 0 2 30 30 30 1
defaultblur 0
defaultopacity 100
defaultColorize 0 0 0 0
defaultHSL 0 0 0
defaultshadow 1 5 5 100 100 75 7.5 0 0 0 1
defaultholdfirst 0 F
defaultholdlast 0 sec
defaultloop 0 3
defaultrandomloop 0 2
defaultsequence 0 5 fwd
defaultrandomstart 0 10 frames

-- Glyphs

glyph "A" "Texture.mov" 720 30
```

Launch the FontMaker module and open up the new script that you've saved. The FontMaker module asks you to place the new texture within a specific category, or you can create a new category. You should now see your new texture within the Media Browser window (see figure 6.5).

LiveFonts vs. standard fonts

In LiveType, the individual characters within a text object are called glyphs. Therefore, when referring to individual characters within the LiveType canvas, I use the term *glyph*.

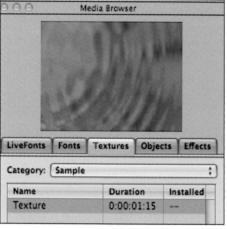

6.5 An animated texture inside the Media Browser window.

Within the Media Browser window are two different font tabs. It is important to differentiate between LiveFonts and standard fonts. The main difference is that LiveFonts are actual animations. Some LiveFonts are designed to be finite in terms of their animation. For example, the Walker LiveFont represents glyphs that walk up to the screen (see figure 6.6). The individual glyphs within the Walker LiveFont aren't really designed to keep looping.

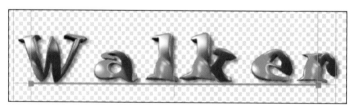

6.6 The Walker LiveFont.

Genius Don't forget, there are two categories within the LiveFonts tab: the Pro Series and the Collectors Edition. You can also purchase additional LiveFonts from www.LiveType Central.com, and they show up as an additional category.

Because LiveFonts are animations, you can adjust the timing of the actual animation. For example, if you take a look at the Freehand LiveFont, you wouldn't want all the glyphs writing on the screen at the same time. This font is designed to write on the screen as if someone were handwriting their name. You cannot adjust the font style of a LiveType because the LiveFont is an actual animation. You can, however, change the color and size of LiveFonts. Each glyph can also be distorted in terms of X, Y, and rotation parameters.

Understanding timing

Timing is the magical parameter that makes LiveType such a wonderful tool. Once you understand how timing works, you can create your own incredible-looking effects that are different from the default templates. Timing is based on a pattern that all things must follow. All you need to do is animate one glyph, and all the other glyphs will follow the same path. This is what makes LiveType so incredible. I've heard many comments from users who have mentioned they could accomplish the same task using After Effects, but it would take much longer without the same amount of control that is available within LiveType.

Genius It is often necessary to hold the last frame of a LiveFont. For example, if you are using the Freehand LiveFont, hold the last frame for a few seconds after all of the characters have written themselves onto the screen. You do this by clicking the Timing tab within the Inspector and adjusting the Hold Last slider to indicate the number of frames to hold last.

Sequence timing

You can use sequence timing to create some incredible effects with minimal effort. For example, you can use timing to create a sweeping glow that travels through each glyph of a title (see figure 6.7).

You can do this entire animation by creating a single keyframe! Keyframes denote a specific action at a specified moment in time and are only available within an effect track. When you create an effect track, the track appears in purple and is always placed underneath a primary track. Each effect track always has a starting keyframe and an ending keyframe. The starting and ending keyframes appear as small, black triangles. If you add additional keyframes, they appear as small, black diamonds.

6.7 Highlighted keyframe for an individual glyph.

Follow these steps to create a glowing sweep that travels through a title.

Genius

The default background in LiveType is set to transparent, which is fine. However, it is sometimes difficult to see certain style elements on a bright background. Therefore, it may be necessary to change the background to black. You do this by choosing Edit menu ⇨ Project Properties. Set the background color to black with an opacity value of 100 percent. Leave the Render Background setting unchecked, which will preserve the transparent background.

1. **Within the Inspector window, type the words** sweeping glow **into the text area.** This automatically creates a new text track within the Timeline window.

2. **Click the Attributes tab within the Inspector window and slide the Color parameter to 100 percent.** This should change your text to blue, as the default color is already set to blue.

3. **Add a new effects track by choosing Track menu ⇨ Add New Effect.** A purple effects track should appear underneath the yellow text track within the Timeline window.

4. **Place the playhead indicator in the middle of the purple effects track.**

5. **Click the Style tab within the Inspector window.** Click the Glow tab and click the Enable check box. This automatically adds a keyframe within the purple effects track based on the placement of your position indicator.

6. **Adjust the Opacity slider to a value of 170 percent, and blur parameters to 20 pixels.** Your title should have a nice, white glow in front of the characters.

Genius

Many sliders within LiveType have a maximum value that you can use with an individual slider. You can manually type in values to have a maximum percentage value up to 999.9 percent.

7. **Within the purple effects track in the timeline, click the first keyframe.** Set the Opacity slider for the Glow to 0 percent. Do the same for the last keyframe.

8. **Click the Timing tab within the Inspector window.** Adjust the Sequence slider to a value of 25 percent, and adjust the Speed slider to 200 percent.

Genius

Each glyph has its own set of keyframes that are exactly the same as all the other glyphs. It is sometimes difficult to click and activate individual keyframes within an effects track. You can use the keyboard shortcut of Option+K to move back to the nearest keyframe. Alternatively, you can use Shift+K to move forward to the nearest keyframe.

That's it! Press the Play button at the bottom of the Canvas window to watch your animation (see figure 6.8).

6.8 An example of a sweeping glow effect in the Canvas window.

Each style has four warp points located in the lower-right corner of the Inspector window. You can create amazing glowing effects by simply dragging the warp points to distort the glow (see figure 6.9). The key to this effect is to keep the position indicator parked on the middle keyframe within an effect track. This way, the glow grows and shrinks back to its original position because the first and last keyframes are set to their original values.

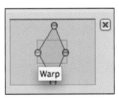

6.9 Warp points for style tab parameters.

Random timing

You can find the Random slider in the Inspector window, under the Timing tab. The Random Timing feature allows glyphs to appear randomly. For example, instead of having each glyph glow from left to right, you can have them randomly glow out of sequence order.

Be careful when using the Random parameter, especially if you have random letters flying on-screen to form a title. Sometimes the random order of characters may accidentally spell something that is offensive to your viewers, by no fault of your own. LiveType provides a random seed parameter to account for this problem. You can experiment with up to 256 different random seeds until you find a random pattern that works.

Using LiveFonts for special effects

In the Media Browser, there is a tab for LiveFonts. Most LiveFonts are very cool, but a few aren't so practical. Three of them in particular — Fogwriter, Oil Fire, and Nitro — appear to be more like animated objects than actual fonts.

Writing in fog

By following these steps, you can use these fonts to create titles that write on the screen with fog:

1. **Type the word** fogwriter **into the text area within the Inspector window.** A new text track appears within the timeline. The track should be yellow, indicating that the layer is a text object.

2. **Click the yellow text track within the Timeline window to make it active.** Then perform a copy and paste to duplicate the track on top of itself (⌘+D for duplicate). When you're finished, click the top track to make it active.

3. **Click the LiveFonts tab within the Media Browser window, and select the Pro Series category from the Category drop-down menu.** Find the Fogwriter font and double-click it. This changes the top track into the Fogwriter LiveFont. Because the Fogwriter font is animated, it has a default length and its text layer automatically extends out. Don't adjust the layer below it just yet.

4. **Play the animation within the LiveType Canvas window.** All the characters on the top layer play as animated fog. The trick is to adjust the timing of the two layers so that the bottom layer fades up in sync with the animated fog.

Depending on the font that you choose, it may be necessary to manually adjust each glyph of the LiveFont so that they line up with the characters below them (see figure 6.10). Within the Canvas window, you can do this by clicking each glyph and carefully aligning its position. It's best to do this before you adjust any timing. When you're done, make sure you deselect any characters you have decided to reposition.

5. **Click the Timing tab within the Inspector window.** Adjust the Sequence slider to a value of 8.0 percent.

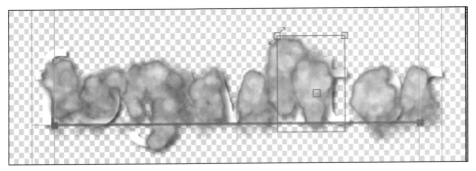

6.10 Lining up Fogwriter glyphs with the layer below.

6. **Within the Timeline window, adjust the length of the bottom text layer to match the fog above it.** The fog should now write each letter individually based on the amount of timing that you've given it. More timing means that it will take a longer time to write out the entire title.

7. **Click the Effects tab within the Media Browser, and click the category drop-down menu to select Fades.** Double-click the Fade-In effect. A purple effects layer is added to the bottom text layer. This purple effects layer has preset keyframes that are required to fade in the layer (Click the top text track, which represents the Fogwriter LiveFont).

8. **Adjust the speed of the effects layer to 50 percent.**

9. **Within the timeline, slide the purple effects layer until the timing of the fog matches the timing of the letters.**

Adjusting glow color

You can change the color of the fog by adding a glow to the LiveFont text layer.

To change the color of the fog, follow these steps:

1. **Click the top text track, which represents the Fogwriter LiveFont.**

2. **Click the Style tab within the Inspector window.**

3. **Enable the glow parameter within the Glow tab (see figure 6.11).**

4. **Choose a color for the glow.**

5. **Adjust the Opacity slider slightly to enhance the texture of the fog.**

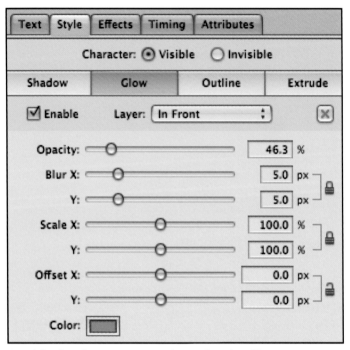

6.11 Adjusting glow parameters to change the color of fog.

Using the Character Palette

LiveType is much more than a title generator; you can use it as a motion graphics tool. LiveType doesn't care whether you're dealing with text or objects. It treats them all the same. Remember, the key function that makes LiveType so incredible is the timing behaviors. You can use timing to create some amazing effects with a small amount of effort.

Genius

From the Character Palette, you can use a variety of shapes from various font sets. These shapes are nothing more than actual fonts. This is a fantastic way to incorporate clip art directly into LiveType.

Assuming you have configured the input menu for the Character Palette (see Chapter 1), you should see your country's flag in the upper-right corner of the Finder.

Follow these steps to create a series of glowing stars:

1. **For viewing purposes, change the background color of the Canvas window to black.**

2. **Place the cursor within the text area of the LiveType Inspector window.**

3. **Click the country flag in the Finder and select Show Character Palette.** The Character Palette dialog opens. Click the Miscellaneous Symbols category (see figure 6.12). Look for the first star symbol that is hollow in the middle. It should be located in the second row, the sixth character to the right. Click the Insert button six times. This places a series of six star characters within the Canvas window of LiveType.

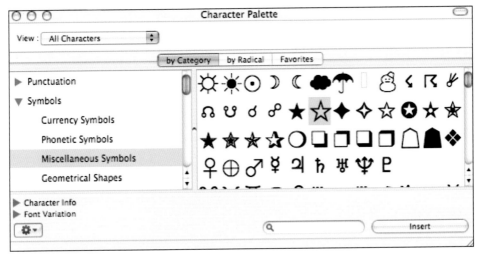

6.12 The Character Palette dialog.

4. **Choose Track menu ⇨ Add New Effect.** This creates a purple effects track for the text layer. It also automatically selects the first keyframe for you. The first keyframe is the small, black triangle within the effects track that is pointing sideways toward the right.

Caution

When adding new effect tracks, it is important that none of the physical characters are selected. Otherwise, the effect only applies to a single glyph.

5. **Select the first white star glyph from the left.** Drag the glyph offscreen outside the canvas area. The other glyphs should follow your same movements.

Genius You can zoom in and out of the visible canvas area by using keyboard shortcuts: ⌘++ for zoom in, or ⌘+- for zoom out.

6. **With the first glyph still selected, increase its size by dragging the upper-right corner of the glyph.** Make it approximately twice its original size.

7. **The upper-left corner of the glyph allows you to rotate the character.** Spin the glyph around 360 degrees (see figure 6.13).

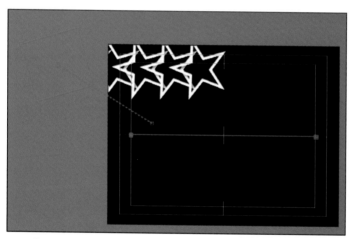

6.13 Changing the glyph parameters within the Canvas window.

8. **Navigate to the Inspector window and click the Attributes tab. Set the opacity to 0 percent.**

9. **Click the Timing tab, and set the sequence timing to 20 percent.**

10. **Add a glow to your existing composite (see figure 6.14) by using the Style tab within the Inspector window.** First, deselect any highlighted glyphs and click the yellow text layer within the Timeline window.

11. **Within the Style tab, click the Glow tab and adjust the parameters.**

12. **Click the Enable check box to activate the glow parameter.**

13. **Set the Layer drop-down menu to Behind.**

14. **Adjust the opacity to 300 percent.** You need to manually enter in this value.

15. **Adjust the blur to 20 pixels or higher.**

16. **Adjust the color to something other than white.**

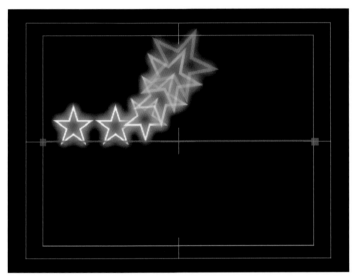

6.14 Adding a glow to all the glyphs.

Caution When adding styles to an entire composite, it is important that you activate the yellow text layer. If the purple effects layer is highlighted, the style is only applied for a particular keyframe at a particular moment in time. It's also important that no actual characters are selected within the Canvas window. Otherwise, the style only applies to a single glyph. An effects track always takes priority over a text track if the same parameter is enabled for both.

Using LiveType for motion graphics compositing

LiveType is also a fantastic tool for motion graphics compositing. If you stick with the idea of using the Character Palette for basic clip art, you can build some amazing composites that use shapes as moving mattes with video inside them.

Using full motion video in LiveType

Follow these steps to matte moving videos inside a series of shapes:

1. **Click inside the text area of the Inspector window, and navigate back to the character map.** Within the character map, find a solid star character. Click the Insert button four times to place the stars inside the Canvas window.

2. **Click the Text tab within the Inspector window, and adjust the size of the stars until they fill the visible screen area.**

Within the Canvas window, you will see two green outlines. These outlines represent the action-safe and title-safe areas of the screen. You should keep any titles safely within the inner green-outlined box to avoid having part of your title cut off when viewed on a television set.

3. **Click the first star or glyph from the left within the Canvas window.** It is critical that you select the first glyph from the left.

4. **Click the Attributes tab within the Inspector window.** Then click the Matte tab.

5. **Click the Matte to: drop-down menu and select Movie or Image.** Click the Choose button and navigate to a QuickTime movie that you've captured using Final Cut Pro. This mattes the movie inside the first glyph. Alternatively, you can matte to a built-in texture.

6. **Slide the Scale slider to 0.0 percent.** This scales the QuickTime movie to fit the shape of the glyph that you have selected. In this case, the movie is scaled to fit inside the star character.

7. **Repeat this process for the three other glyphs using a different video file or texture.**

Caution The Scale slider is grayed out and unavailable if you do not click the first glyph from the left.

To further enhance the matte shapes, you can add a glow to all of the characters. To do this, make sure all the characters have been deselected.

1. **Navigate to the Style tab within the Inspector window.** Click the Glow tab and click the Enable check box.

2. **Set the Layer drop-down menu to Behind.**

3. **Change the Opacity and Blur sliders to give your characters a nice glow.**

As you can see in figure 6.15, this produces an amazing effect. Although a similar effect can be done with Apple Motion, I think you'll agree that effects like this are incredibly easy to do directly within LiveType.

6.15 Four glyphs with video matted inside them.

Text on a curve

LiveType makes it easy to type and animate text on a curve. For example, you can create an animation where the characters spin around the edge of a circle. A track curve is represented by a blue line underneath a text object. By default, a track curve always starts out as a straight line. You can change the curve by right-clicking directly on the track curve within the Canvas window. This produces a contextual menu that allows you to add a control point (see figure 6.16).

Follow the steps below to create a track curve in the form of a circle.

1. **Navigate to the Inspector window and type the words** 'text on a curve' **within the text area.** This creates a yellow text track in the Timeline window.

2. **Add three control points within the blue track curve.** You should now have a total of five points, including the first and last points.

6.16 Adding a control point.

3. **Drag the starting and ending control points to the upper edge of the Canvas window.** You'll attach these two loose points together as part of the last step. Drag the other three points to the left, right, and bottom edges of the Canvas window. The idea here is to form a diamond.

4. **Right-click each control point again and choose Curve In and Curve Out for each point (see figure 6.17).** These curves are called Bezier curves. You can use these curves to change the diamond path into a circle path.

5. **For the ending and starting point, you only have one choice (either Curve In or Curve Out).**

6. **Extend the Bezier curves on the handles so that they are an equal distance on all of the sides within the Canvas window.**

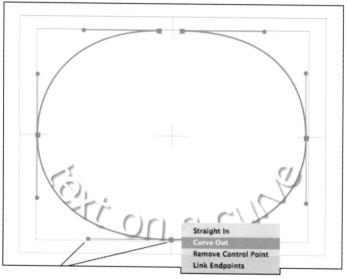

6.17 Adjusting Bezier curves.

7. **At the top of the canvas, attach the two points together so they connect.**

The next series of steps is to animate the text so that it moves around the circle.

1. **Navigate to the Effects tab within the Media Browser and choose the Motion Path category from the Category drop-down menu.** Double-click the effect preset called Slide-left 100%. Notice that the text now flies in from the left side of the screen and follows the track curve. If you want the text to travel completely around the circle, you need to link the start and end points together.

2. **Right-click the starting or ending point toward the top of the canvas, and choose Link Endpoints.** Now the entire animation follows around the circle. The last step is to have the characters fade in over time.

3. **Click the first keyframe within the purple effect tracks for any character.** Adjust the opacity to 0 percent.

As you can see, certain adjustments can create an entirely different look. For this reason, LiveType is an amazing title tool.

Exporting from LiveType

When you're ready to output, you have two basic choices: You can save a self-contained QuickTime movie, or you can drag the LiveType project icon directly into Final Cut Pro. There are advantages and disadvantages to both methods.

If you choose to render a self-contained movie, the process is simple. Choose File menu ⇨ Render Movie. Then select a destination to save your movie. The advantage of this method is that you can use this rendered movie anywhere you choose. You could take the movie with you to another Final Cut Pro system or send the file to someone else for use within another software program.

The second option is to drag the LiveType project icon directly from LiveType into Final Cut Pro (see figure 6.18). To do this, you must first save your LiveType project. Once the project has been saved, you can see an incredibly small T icon at the very top of the Canvas window. I recommend sliding the Canvas window slightly to the left and then dragging the T icon from the LiveType Canvas window directly into the Final Cut Pro browser window.

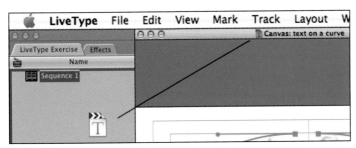

6.18 Dragging the LiveType project icon into the Final Cut Pro browser window.

The advantage of using this method is two-fold. First, there is no rendering time. A graphic clip automatically appears within the Final Cut Pro browser window, and you can immediately edit that clip to the Final Cut Pro timeline.

Second, the clip is now linked to the actual LiveType project. This means that if you need to make a change to the title, all you need to do is right-click the graphic within the Final Cut Pro timeline and select Open in Editor (see figure 6.19). This automatically relaunches LiveType with the associated project. You can make changes to the LiveType project and resave it; the changes automatically update within the Final Cut Pro timeline.

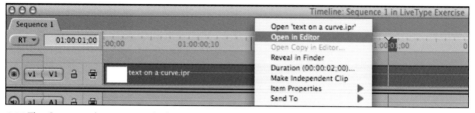

6.19 The Contextual menu reveals the Open in Editor function.

Boris Title 3D

Boris Title 3D is an integrated plug-in found within the Final Cut Pro Generators menu. It is the best choice for designing basic titles among the 12 different title tools available to Final Cut Pro users. Mastering the basics of the Title 3D title tool is fairly easy. However, there are some interesting tricks that many users miss out on.

First off, where exactly are the 3D attributes for building titles? The term *Title 3D* can be a bit misleading. The Title 3D tool doesn't actually render anything in true 3D space. It simulates titles that look 3D by adding a solid drop shadow. Title 3D adds a bit of lighting that fools the eye into thinking the characters are truly 3D.

Follow these steps to create a simulated 3D title.

1. **Launch the Title 3D title tool by choosing Generators menu ➪ Boris ➪ Title 3D.** The Generators menu is located in the bottom-right corner of the Viewer window. It looks like the letter A.

2. **Click the Controls tab within the Viewer window, and then click the Title 3D button near the top of the Viewer window where it says 'Click for options.'** This launches the Title 3D plug-in.

Genius

Title 3D supports up to five different drop shadows! The important thing here is to make sure that you are working with one drop shadow at a time.

3. **Type your title within the Canvas area of the Title 3D window.** Highlight all the characters by using the keyboard shortcut (Ctrl+A).

4. **In the lower-left corner of the Title 3D window, click the Drop Shadow tool.**

5. **Pull down the Shadow Type drop-down menu and select Solid Shadow (see figure 6.20).**

6. **Adjust the shadow opacity, distance, and angle to configure the 3D look of your title.** It's best if you adjust the shadow opacity to 100 percent for the best 3D look.

When you're finished, don't forget to deselect your characters in order to see the true look of your finished composite.

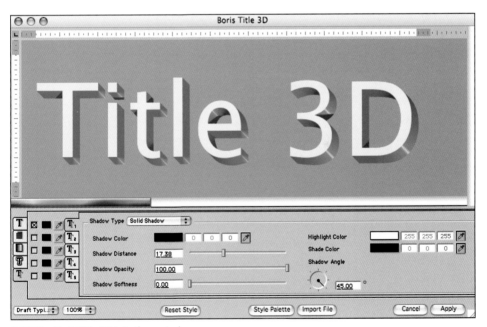

6.20 The Boris Title 3D interface window.

Building Titles in Photoshop

With the Photoshop CS series, you can build titles using nonsquare pixels. You do not need to worry about the relationship between square and nonsquare pixels when working with NTSC video.

Here are a couple of key tips that make your life easier when incorporating Photoshop elements into Final Cut Pro:

- Build your images on a transparent background.
- Change the Pixel Aspect Ratio that is compatible with the video format that you are working with.
- Use the PNG file format when saving your final image.
- Save an additional PSD copy for changes that require manipulation of original Photoshop layers.

Genius

The PNG format is an easy format to use to ensure maximum compatibility with Final Cut Pro.

Among the really cool features offered in Photoshop are the various layer styles that you can apply to images (see figure 6.21). However, Final Cut Pro does not correctly understand Photoshop layer styles, and so it simply ignores them.

Therefore, you need to flatten and merge all the layer styles into a normal layer. Instead of going through all those steps, it is much easier to save your final image as a PNG file, which accomplishes the same thing. Keep a PSD copy nearby, just in case you need to make changes to the original layer styles within Photoshop.

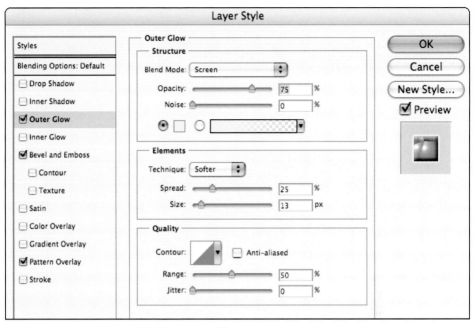

6.21 The Layer Style menu within Photoshop CS3.

Improving the Quality of Graphics and Titles

If you are using LiveType to build your titles, the only export option uses the Animation codec, which is an uncompressed codec. This means that any titles that you save directly out of LiveType are uncompressed, based on whatever resolution you have chosen in the LiveType project preferences.

Genius

Fortunately, you can change your sequence settings to an uncompressed codec before you output your final QuickTime movie. This gives you the best-quality movie before you begin the DVD creation process.

125

For Final Cut Pro users, the real problem lies within the Final Cut Pro sequence settings. Unfortunately for many users, the default sequence settings within Final Cut Pro are set to NTSC-DV. If you are working with DV media within Final Cut Pro, your uncompressed titles are rerendered and compressed to a ratio of 5:1.

Follow these steps to change your sequence settings.

1. **Find your sequence within the Final Cut Pro browser window.** Right-click your sequence and choose Settings from the contextual menu. This opens the Sequence Settings dialog.

2. **Change the QuickTime Video Settings Compressor drop-down menu to Animation.**

3. **Output a QuickTime movie by choosing File menu ⇨ Export ⇨ QuickTime.** Make sure that the Make Movie Self-Contained check box is selected.

How Can I Use Final Cut Pro for High-End Effects Compositing?

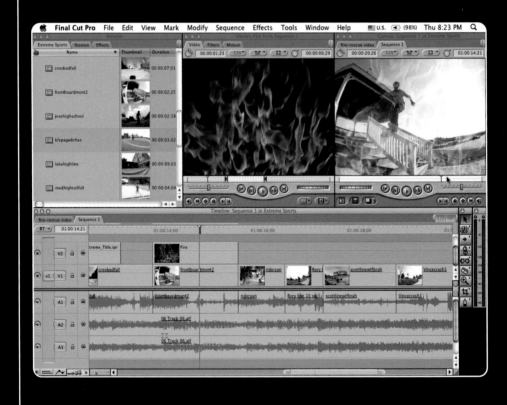

Final Cut Pro provides some fantastic effects-compositing tools. The catch is learning what type of effects Final Cut Pro is good at. With certain effects, you may be better off passing them into Apple Motion. This section focuses on practical effects that you can create directly within the Final Cut Pro interface.

Installing Third-Party Effects

Final Cut Pro supports a variety of third-party effects. Better yet, there are individuals who have written free plug-ins that you can download and use. One such Web site is www.mattias.nu/plugins/. This site provides a set of plug-ins called Too Much Too Soon (see figure 7.1).

Caution I recommend installing any third-party effects in the following location: Mac HD ⇨ Library ⇨ Application Support ⇨ Final Cut Pro System Support ⇨ Plugins. This way, the plug-ins will be available to any Mac OS X user who launches Final Cut Pro. After installing plug-ins, you need to restart Final Cut Pro in order for the software to recognize them.

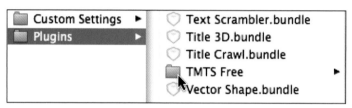

7.1 The Too Much Too Soon plug-ins installed.

To keep all your plug-ins organized, you can place the entire folder inside the Plugins folder.

Creating Freeze Frame Effects

Creating a freeze frame is quite easy: Park over any frame within a sequence and press Shift+N. This places a freeze frame of the clip into the Viewer window. Unless you've changed your still/duration freeze frame preferences, you end up with a freeze frame that has 10 seconds of duration marked in the middle of the clip.

Caution If you have multiple video layers stacked on top of each other and you perform a freeze frame function, Final Cut Pro creates a freeze frame of the top-most visible layer.

As a practical exercise, you can use a freeze frame to create a special effect that freezes the action in the middle of a clip. Just follow these steps:

1. **Edit a clip to a new sequence that contains some action.** Place the playhead indicator at the point where you want to freeze the action.

2. **Create a freeze frame of that point in time by using the keyboard shortcut Shift+N.** This places a freeze frame in the Viewer window.

3. **Specify a duration of 1:00 instead of the default 10:00 value for the freeze frame that is in the Viewer window.**

4. **Press the yellow Insert button located in the Canvas window or press F9 (see figure 7.2).** This splices in a 1:00 freeze frame in the middle of the clip that is in the Timeline.

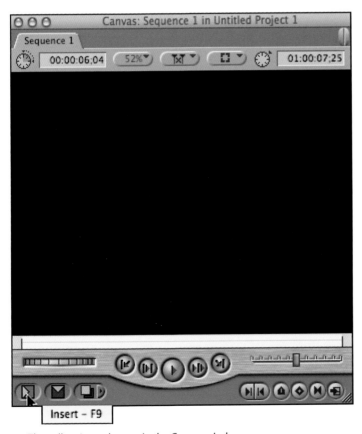

7.2 The yellow Insert button in the Canvas window.

You can polish up this effect by adding a dip-to-color transition and a camera flash sound effect at the transition point. In figure 7.3, I'm using the free Flashframe transition, which is from the Too Much Too Soon pack of filters. Alternatively, although not quite as cool, you could create something similar by creating a dip-to-white transition at the transition point.

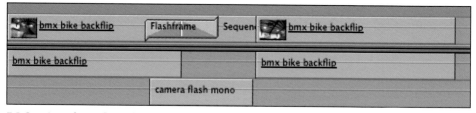

7.3 Creating a freeze frame flash effect.

Remember, you have access to thousands of sound effects that are available with Soundtrack Pro. Make sure you review how to configure the Spotlight feature of Mac OS X to search for sound effects that are installed on your hard drive.

Slow Motion Effects

There are two types of slow motion effects: constant and variable speeds. Fortunately, Final Cut Pro makes it incredibly easy to create these types of motion effects.

Constant speed motion effects

Constant slow motion is quite easy to understand. Constant speed means that the speed change remains constant. For example, if you slow something down to 50 percent normal speed, it stays that way through the duration of the clip. You can also click the Reverse check box, which makes a clip play in reverse. You can even play a clip in slow-motion reverse.

You can slow down an original master clip that resides in the Browser window, or directly slow down a clip that's already in the Timeline. It is common practice to apply speed changes directly within the Timeline window.

To slow down a master clip prior to editing it to a sequence, follow these steps:

1. **Double-click the clip in the Browser window.** This loads its contents into the Viewer window.

2. **Click Modify ⇨ Speed and specify a speed change value.**

The master clip inherits the new speed characteristics. If you want to undo the process, you can repeat these same steps and change the speed value back to 100 percent. It is important to note that speed changes also affect audio. Changing the speed of audio effectively changes its pitch.

Caution

If you choose to slow down a master clip, the speed change stays with the clip until you change it back. This may lead to a bit of confusion if you plan on using the clip for normal editing purposes. I therefore recommend making a copy of the clip in the Browser window and renaming the clip to signify that it has a speed change.

To slow down a clip directly within the Timeline window, all you need to do is right-click a specific clip and choose Speed from the contextual pop-up menu. Then enter a speed percentage and click OK.

Caution

When you slow a clip down directly in the Timeline window, Final Cut Pro extends or shortens the length of your sequence based on the speed change that you specify.

Creating a speed change special effect

While I am on the subject of creating slow motion effects, let me point out that it is very easy to create a special effect where the speed of a clip suddenly changes (slows down) and then resumes normal speed. This is a common visual effect that you can see in sports and music videos.

Here's how it is done:

1. **Edit a clip to an empty sequence, preferably a clip that has some sort of action.** For example, if a clip shows an athlete slam-dunking a basketball, during the slam dunk, you can create an effect where the clip slows down and then resumes normal speed.

2. **Use the Blade tool to mark two edit points so that you have a new clip area between the actions that you want to slow down.** You now have three pieces of the clip. The idea here is to slow down the middle section of the clip that contains the physical action.

3. **Right-click the middle section of the clip and choose Speed from the contextual menu (see figure 7.4).** Type in a value of 50 percent. Final Cut Pro automatically extends the length of the sequence to make room for the slower section in the middle. That's it! It doesn't get any easier than that.

7.4 Adjusting the speed of a clip in the Timeline.

Variable speed motion effects

Variable speed means you can have a speed ramp. In other words, you can have a clip start at 0 percent speed and ramp up to 100 percent, or vice versa. This type of effect is often done with music videos.

The one difficult fact to grasp about performing a variable speed effect is that the actual clip's duration does not change. This means that if you slow down the beginning of a clip, you need to speed up the end of the clip to make up for the time lost. Or, as another example, if you slow down the middle section of a clip, you need to speed up the beginning and ending sections of the clip. It gets even crazier if you play a part of the clip in reverse, because you then really have to speed things up to catch up with the clip's timing.

There are several ways to create a variable slow-motion effect. I'll focus on what I believe is the easiest method, which involves building the effect directly within the Timeline window.

Follow these steps to create a basic variable slow-motion effect:

1. **Find a clip within a sequence that contains some action.**

2. **Click the Toggle Clip Keyframes button (see figure 7.5).** This button is located in the bottom-left corner of the Timeline window. The Timeline tracks expand to reveal an area for plotting keyframes, along with speed indicators underneath each track.

7.5 The Toggle Clip Keyframes button.

3. **Activate the Time Remap tool (see figure 7.6).** The Time Remap tool is located in the tool palette. Chances are that the tool is hidden underneath the Slip tool. The Time Remap tool looks like a stopwatch.

4. **Place two keyframes within the keyframe editor using the Time Remap tool.** When adding keyframes with the Time Remap tool, click directly onto the clip itself. Each time you click within the clip area, a new keyframe is added to the blue motion bar (see figure 7.7).

5. **Adjust the timing between keyframes to change the motion parameters.** For example, by dragging the two keyframes further apart, you are adjusting the timing between those two points in time. This means that the clip plays slower in the middle portion and faster at the beginning and ending. The speed indicators below the track show the timing difference between individual keyframes (see figure 7.8).

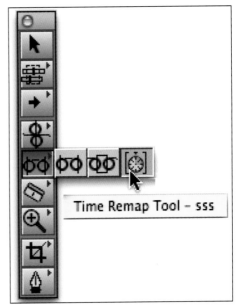

7.6 The Time Remap tool.

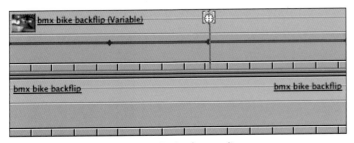

7.7 Adding motion keyframes in the keyframe editor area.

7.8 Changing speed timing by adjusting keyframes.

Caution

When using variable slow motion, the audio is not affected by the variable speed changes. If your clip has associated audio, the audio drifts in and out of synch.

Playing clips in reverse with variable motion

You can even use the variable slow motion to make a video clip dance. This means that you can adjust the keyframing of a clip's motion to create a video mix that goes in synch with the music. This effect represents a new trend in some dance clubs, where music videos are preproduced and reedited to play in synch with the music beat.

To create this type of effect, follow these steps:

1. **Create a variable motion effect.** See the previous exercise for more detail on how to perform that effect.

2. **Expand the keyframe area by adjusting the keyframe editor size (see figure 7.9).** Click off to the side of the sequence to expand its size.

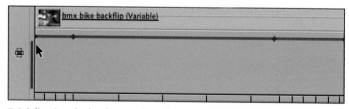

7.9 Adjusting the keyframe editor size.

3. **Right-click in the keyframe editor area and choose Time Remap ⇨ Time Graph from the contextual menu (see figure 7.10).** This displays a time graph based on the keyframes that you have placed. The graph moves upward, which indicates the motion of the clip if moving forward in time.

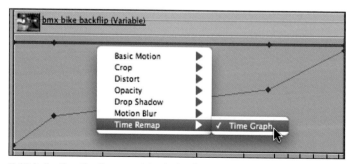

7.10 Activating the time graph in the keyframe area.

136

4. **Adjust one of the keyframes downward below the position of a previous keyframe (see figure 7.11).** This causes the motion to play backward based on that point in time. Be careful not to drag the position of the keyframe too far down. Drag the keyframe slightly below the position of the previous keyframe. When you see the slope of the keyframe graph moving downward, this indicates that the clip will be playing backward. Red tick marks in the timing area also help to indicate backward motion.

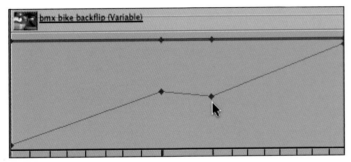

7.11 Adjusting the keyframe graph to play motion backward.

Note The keyframe graph for variable slow motion effects can be quite confusing at first. Points in time are measured by where keyframes are within the y axis (meaning up or down). A keyframe at the top of the graph indicates that you are at the last frame of a clip. A keyframe at the bottom of the graph indicates that you are at the first frame of a clip. The slope of the graph indicates how fast the clip is moving; the steeper the slope, the faster the motion.

Creating a smooth motion graph

You can also create a smooth graph for individual keyframes by right-clicking a keyframe and choosing Smooth from the contextual menu (see figure 7.12). Adjust these Bezier handles to smooth out the motion path. You can also clear a keyframe by using the same contextual menu.

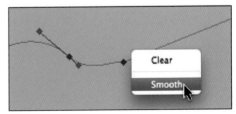

7.12 Smoothing out the time graph.

137

Understanding Composite Modes

Using composite modes is at the core of being able to design complex visual effects. Graphic designers may be familiar with the use of composite modes for photos and still images. In Final Cut Pro, a composite mode tells a video layer how to react with a video layer below it.

Take a look at figure 7.13. If you have a video clip that is on V2 with the contents (in this case, fire) placed over a background on V1, you can create a visual composite by changing the composite mode that will react with the layer below it. For example, if you change the composite mode to Screen, Final Cut Pro uses the clip on V1 to multiply the inverse of the colors below. This brightens the image based on the areas of the fire, producing a visual effect that looks like the skateboarder is jumping through a wall of fire.

7.13 Composite mode screen.

To change a clip's composite mode, right-click a clip and choose Composite Mode from the contextual menu (see figure 7.14). You'll notice a variety of choices that are explained below. Each composite mode has its own algorithm in terms of how clips react to each other.

138

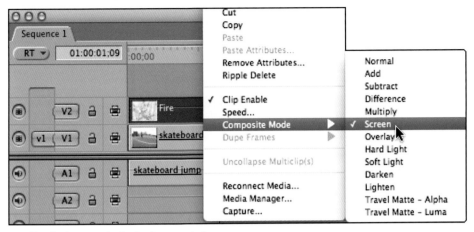

7.14 The final composite in the Canvas window.

You have to experiment with the various composite modes, as they all do something different. The important thing to remember is that the composite mode is always changed on the top clip, and it always reacts with the clip directly below it. Table 7.1 explains the actions of some composite modes.

Table 7.1 Composite Modes

Mode	Action
Add	Combines the color values of the top clips, producing a lighter image.
Subtract	Produces a darker image because color values are subtracted from each other.
Difference	Subtracts colors on V1 from V2.
Multiply	Multiplies the color values of the pixels together, often producing a much darker image.
Screen	The reverse of Multiply. Multiplies the inverse value of the colors on V1 and V2, producing a lighter image.
Overlay	A combination of Multiply and Screen. For any color values over 128, the Screen mode is applied, making this section of the image brighter. For color values under 128, the Multiply mode is applied, making that part of the image darker.
Hard Light	Makes light areas lighter and dark areas darker. It leaves a hard edge between dark and light areas.
Soft light	Similar to the Hard Light. Diffuses the transition between dark and light areas, leaving a soft transition between the two.
Darken	Compares the values of the two clips and chooses the darker values.
Lighten	Compares the values of the two clips and chooses the lighter values.

Notice there is no direct control over each composite mode. However, by adjusting a clip's opacity using the clip overlays, you can actively change how a composite mode reacts with the clip below it (see figure 7.15).

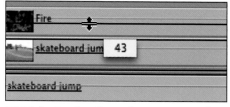

The Travel Matte–Alpha composite mode

7.15 Adjusting the clip overlay transparency line to affect the composite mode.

The composite mode, Travel Matte–Alpha, is incredibly important when it comes to building complex composites. This mode allows Final Cut Pro to composite video inside of any shape, graphic, or title that contains an alpha channel.

You can easily see whether a clip contains an alpha channel by choosing Checkerboard 1 or Checkerboard 2 from the View drop-down menu at the top of the Viewer window (see figure 7.16). If you see a black-and-white checkerboard pattern behind your title, that title contains an alpha channel.

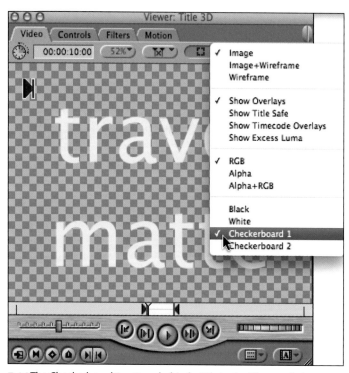

7.16 The Checkerboard 1 pattern behind a title in the Viewer window.

To composite video into a shape or title that contains an alpha channel, follow these steps:

1. **Edit a shape or graphic onto V1 that contains an alpha channel.**

2. **Place a video clip directly above the graphic onto V2.**

Genius

Instead of dragging a clip onto V2 and then trimming its contents to match V1, use the Superimpose feature to automatically place a clip onto V2 that matches the duration of the clip that's on V1. Park the playhead indicator over the top of the clip that's on V1 and press the Superimpose button or F12 to automatically superimpose it onto V2.

The Superimpose button is hidden underneath the Replace button in the Canvas window. Hold down your mouse button on the Replace button until a subset of new buttons appears. You can then click the Superimpose button (see figure 7.17).

7.17 Using the Superimpose function.

3. **Right-click the clip that's on V2.** Select Composite Mode ⇨ Travel Matte–Alpha from the contextual menu (see figure 7.18).

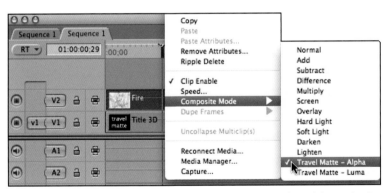

7.18 Compositing the fire clip title by clicking Composite Mode and then selecting Travel Matte-Alpha.

Caution When you use the Travel Matte – Alpha composite mode, Final Cut Pro completely ignores the contents of the shape or graphic. In other words, Final Cut Pro fills the graphic with whatever video is on V2, regardless of color. It also replaces any edges or drop shadows with the video that's on V2. Bottom line, when using the Travel Matte – Alpha composite mode, the only thing that is important is the shape, because the entire shape is filled with what's on V2.

The video content of V2 is now placed inside the title on V1 (see figure 7.19).

7.19 Viewing the final composite in the Canvas window.

To create a travel matte that contains a drop shadow or edge, you need additional video layers. For example, let's say you want to create a title that contains moving fire, but you also want the title to have a beveled edge.

Follow these steps to create the effect:

1. **Use the Boris Title 3D title tool to create a large, plain-looking title.** Create the title large enough to fill the entire screen. Do not create any edges or drop shadows for the title.

2. **Edit the title to V1.**

3. **Superimpose a clip onto V2.** This example uses a clip containing fire.

4. **Use the Travel Matte – Alpha composite mode to superimpose V2 into the title on V1.**

5. **Move both layers up a layer to the clips that reside on V3 and V2, leaving an empty layer on V1 (see figure 7.20).**

7.20 Move both layers up a layer.

The trick is to make an exact copy of the title below itself. Then add the beveled edge to the title on the bottom. The title on the bottom sticks out from the title above it, creating the effect of having a beveled title with fire inside the letters.

6. **Hold down the Option and Shift keys, and drag the title from V2 to V1 (see figure 7.21).** This makes an exact copy of the title underneath itself.

7.21 Duplicate the title onto a layer below itself.

7. **Add an edge and/or drop shadow to the title on V1.** You need to double-click the title to reload it back into the Viewer window in order to relaunch the title into Boris 3D. Then you can make changes by adding a border or bevel (see figure 7.22).

7.22 The title is filled with fire and also has a beveled edge.

The Travel Matte–Luma composite mode

The Travel Matte–Luma composite mode works very similarly to the Travel Matte–Alpha composite mode. The main difference is that Final Cut Pro uses the luminance values to determine which area to key out. Areas that are not 100-percent white become transparent based on the amount of luminance. This means that a matte that is gray would be 50 percent transparent.

Can I Use Final Cut Pro to Produce Complex Motion Effects?

Final Cut Pro provides amazing functionality when it comes to working with basic motion. With so much power available, it's easy to get carried away and fall into complex traps that eat away at your valuable time. Building motion effects within Final Cut Pro should be a seamless process. In this chapter, I share some incredible tips and tricks that will save you countless hours when building your composites. It's important to optimize your workflow and increase your efficiency so the software doesn't interfere with your creativity.

Working with the Motion Tab

The Motion tab provides core functionality in terms of moving video elements around within the video frame. At first glance, the interface may seem similar to other programs such as Adobe After Effects. The default location of the Motion tab is within the Viewer window.

The Motion tab provides the critical functions in the following list. In the next sections, I provide extra detail for Drop Shadow and Opacity.

- Basic Motion
- Crop
- Distort
- Opacity
- Drop Shadow
- Motion Blur
- Time Remap

Adding a drop shadow

Within the Motion tab, you can easily add a drop shadow to any graphic element that contains an alpha channel. You can also add a drop shadow to a clip that has been scaled down to be a picture-in-picture. Adding a drop shadow typically improves your titles or graphics by adding a sense of depth to them.

Follow these steps to add a drop shadow to a clip:

1. **Double click on a title or graphic within the Timeline window.** This will load its contents into the Viewer window.
2. **Click on the Motion tab.**
3. **Click on the Drop Shadow check box to activate a drop shadow (see figure 8.1).**
4. **Click on the disclosure triangle to reveal the drop shadow controls.** You can change the drop shadow parameters to affect how your drop shadow looks.

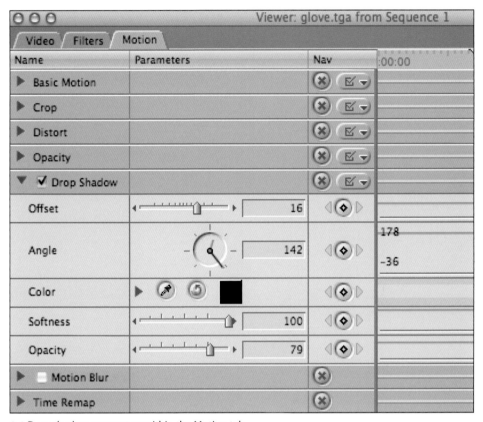

8.1 Drop shadow parameters within the Motion tab.

Take a look at the difference between the two clips in figure 8.2. Notice how the drop shadow helps the graphic pop out from the screen.

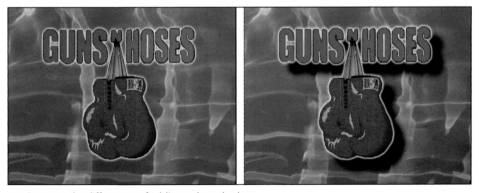

8.2 Compare the differences of adding a drop shadow.

Changing clip opacity

Changing a clip's opacity value is also a function of the Motion tab.. Changing something as simple as a clip's opacity can be an effective tool for creating visual effects.

You can also adjust opacity directly in the Timeline. You can do this by clicking on the Toggle Clip Overlays button located in the bottom-left corner of the Timeline window. This button looks like a mountain peak (see figure 8.3).

8.3 Toggle clip overlay button.

Turning on the clip overlays enables you to easily control a clip's opacity directly within the Timeline. After you click on the Toggle Clip Overlays button, a black line appears at the top of all the video clips within the Timeline window (see figure 8.4). You can drag the black clip-overlay line until you achieve the desired opacity level.

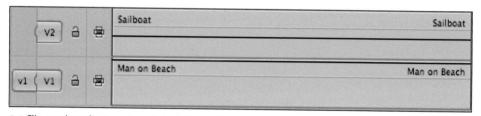

8.4 Clip overlay adjustment made in Sailboat clip.

As you can see in figure 8.5, a shot of a lonely guy at the beach definitely has a different feel when you composite in a shot of a sailboat. I lowered the opacity of the sailboat shot to achieve this effect.

You can create variable opacity levels to ramp the opacity up or down by holding down the Option key and clicking on the clip overlay line. This creates keyframes. To create a ramp, you need at least two keyframes.

8.5 Lowered opacity on Sailboat clip.

Adding Motion with Keyframes

You can create amazing composites by assigning keyframes to various clip elements. A keyframe represents a moment in time and is represented by a small diamond within each parameter (see figure 8.6). You can assign motion parameters such as position, scale, and rotation to individual keyframes. This allows you to have motion parameters change over time based on the value assigned to each keyframe.

The key to creating great-looking effects is in the timing of how elements appear and disappear on the screen. The idea is to create a motion path for one clip and then copy all the keyframes to other clips to create a unique composite. The last step involves using multiple video layers to create a sense of visual timing.

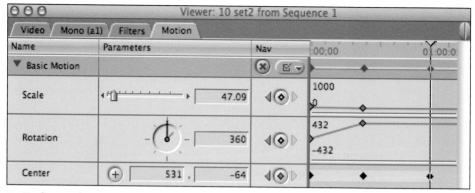

8.6 Keyframes placed within the Motion tab.

You can tear the Motion tab off from the Viewer window and place it as a tab within the Timeline window. This gives you added space in terms of screen area when adding keyframes and plotting motion paths. Since the Timeline window typically stretches across the bottom of the screen, placing the Motion tab in the Timeline window provides you an extended work area when building your motion effects (see figure 8.7). When you're finished, you can right-click on the Motion tab and close it. It will reappear in the Viewer window.

Genius

When working with keyframes in Final Cut Pro, edit your clip to the Timeline and then double-click it within the Timeline window. Make sure the playhead indicator is parked over the clip that you are adjusting. This allows you to view changes within the Canvas window as you make adjustments within the Motion tab. Otherwise, you have to switch back and forth between the Motion tab and the Video tab to see your results.

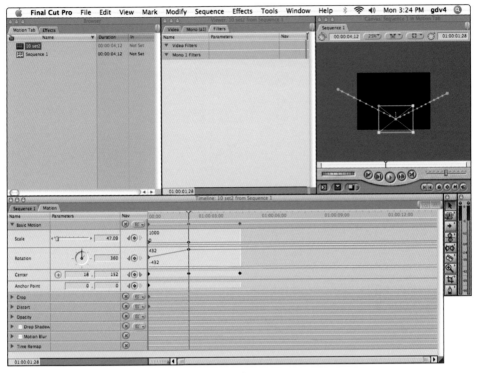

8.7 Motion tab placed within the Timeline window for extra room.

Using Image+Wireframe mode

Most users may be familiar with using the Motion tab and/or the Image + Wireframe mode within the Canvas window to plot all their keyframes. A combination of these methods provides an excellent way to visualize what is going to happen as you place your keyframes.

Follow these steps to create a basic motion path while using Image+Wireframe mode:

1. **Create a new sequence and edit a single clip to the Timeline window.** Preferably, use a 3-second clip.

2. **Place the playhead indicator over the first frame of the clip within the Timeline window and double-click on the clip.** This loads the clip's contents in the Viewer window.

3. **Click on the View Pop-Up window within the Canvas window and select Image + Wireframe (see figure 8.8).**

8.8 View pop-up menu.

4. **Click the Zoom Pop-Up menu within the Canvas window and set the zoom to 50% or less (see figure 8.9).** Alternatively, you can use the keyboard shortcuts of ⌘++ or ⌘+- to zoom in or out of the Canvas window.

5. **Click on the Motion tab within the Viewer window.** Adjust the Scale slider to 50%. If the playhead indicator is parked over the clip within the Timeline window, the Canvas window gives you the results of your video as you adjust the slider.

6. **Move the playhead indicator to the first frame of the clip within the Timeline window.**

7. **Drag the wireframe of the clip so it starts at the left edge of the visible picture area within the Canvas window.**

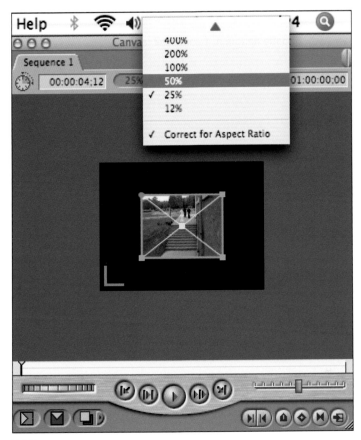

8.9 Zoom pop-up menu.

8. **Click on the Add Motion Keyframe button within the Canvas window.** After you've set the first keyframe, new keyframes are automatically created based on the position of the playhead indicator anytime you move the wireframe. The wireframe area of the video clip turns green to signify that a keyframe has been set at that particular point in time (see figure 8.10).

Genius When adjusting sliders for a motion parameter, you can use your mouse's scroll wheel or your roller ball to roll the slider increments by a value of +/- 1. If you hold down the Option key while using the scroll wheel, the slider increments change by a value of +/- 10.

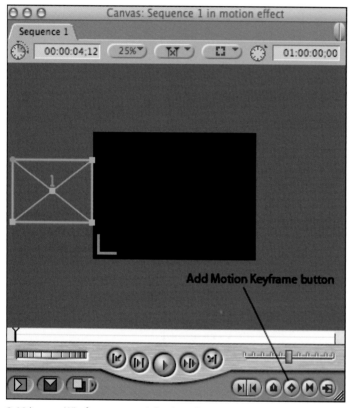

8.10 Image+Wireframe area at left edge of the screen.

9. **Move the playhead indicator forward 1.5 seconds and drag the wireframe area of the clip toward the bottom center area of the screen.** Notice that a new keyframe has been created at this new position (see figure 8.11).

156

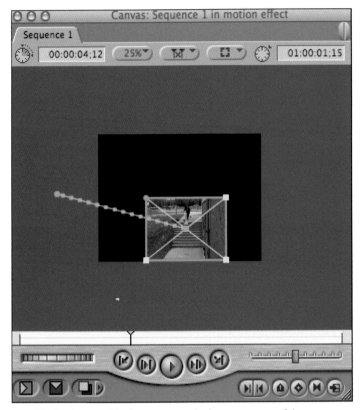

8.11 Moving Image+Wireframe area to the bottom center of the screen.

10. **Move the playhead indicator to the last frame of the clip and drag the wireframe area off to the right side of the Canvas window.** Play the clip. You should see your clip bounce across the Canvas window.

When moving to the last frame of a clip, make sure you are really on the last frame. It is a common mistake to plot keyframes outside the visible clip area. An angled bracket in the lower-right corner of the visible frame within the Canvas window signifies that you are parked on the last frame of a clip (see figure 8.12).

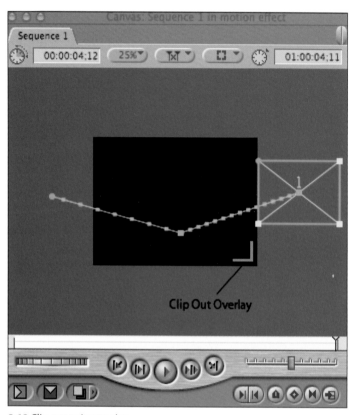

8.12 Clip out point overlay.

Plotting keyframes

A lot of Final Cut Pro users struggle with manipulating keyframes. I've found this can be quite easy when I use the Image+Wireframe mode in conjunction with a couple of keyboard shortcuts.

Use the Add Motion Keyframe button within the Canvas window or the keyboard shortcut Ctrl+K to automatically enable all available motion keyframes. This makes the keyframing process much easier. To jump forward to the next keyframe, use the keyboard shortcut Shift+K. To move backward to the next keyframe, use Option+K.

Genius

You can use the exercise in the section "Using Image+Wireframe mode" and the same basic concept discussed there to plot paths for any clip element.

Working with Bezier curves

When the Image+Wireframe mode is turned on within the Canvas window, a visual path displays based on keyframes that have been created. Small green dots within the path represent keyframes. You will notice from the previous exercise that the default path is somewhat rigid when moving around corners. You can smooth out the corners by using something called Bezier curves.

You can turn on Bezier curves by right-clicking on a green dot and choosing either Ease In/Ease Out or Linear from the contextual menu (see figure 8.13). You are now able to drag the Bezier curve handles to create a curved path. Notice that both handles move together.

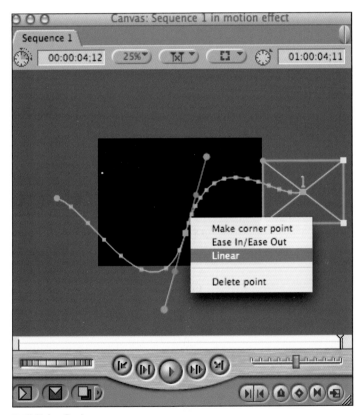

8.13 Using Bezier curves.

The speed of the motion path is determined by tick marks. You can adjust the velocity handles to change the Ease In/Ease Out values (see figure 8.14). The distance between the tick marks indicates the speed of the motion path. If the tick marks are further away from each other, the clip must travel faster between them. If the tick marks are closer together, the clip moves slower between them.

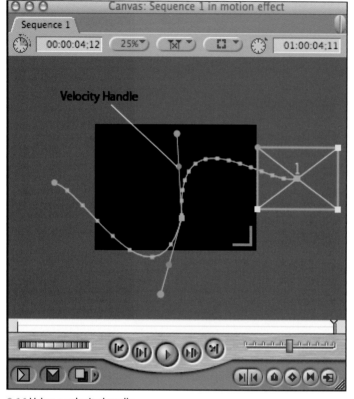

8.14 Using a velocity handle.

Genius

Hold down Ú+Shift while dragging a handle to move one particular handle without affecting the other.

Saving motion favorites

You can save a favorite motion effect by navigating to the Effects menu ➪ Make Favorite Motion. You can have as many favorite motions as you'd like. You can also map your favorite motions to shortcuts on the keyboard. However, you can only map the first nine favorite motions to a key.

To map a favorite motion to a keyboard shortcut command, follow these steps:

1. **Navigate to the Tools menu ➪ Keyboard Layout ➪ Customize.** This opens the Keyboard Layout window (see figure 8.15).

2. **In the upper-right corner of the Keyboard Layout window, type the keywords** motion path **into the search box.** A list of Motion Path Favorites appears. The first four motion paths already have default keyboard shortcuts assigned to them.

3. **Unlock the Keyboard Layout by clicking on the lock in the bottom-left corner of the Keyboard Layout window.**

4. **Drag the appropriate favorite motion to a shortcut key.**

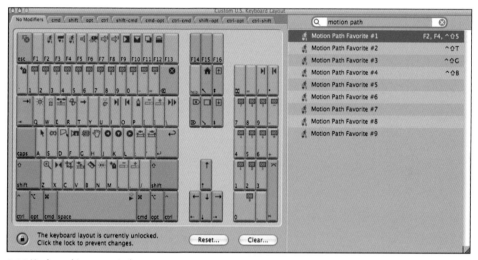

8.15 Keyboard Layout window.

Genius

I recommend that you create your own shortcuts to help with your memory.

Organizing motion favorites

You can apply favorite motions by simply pressing the shortcut key while the playhead indicator is parked over an individual clip. If the playhead indicator is parked over multiple clips within the Timeline window, Final Cut Pro applies the same favorite motion to all the clips based on the auto-select icons within the Timeline window (see figure 8.16).

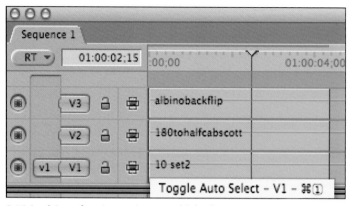

8.16 Applying a favorite motion to multiple clips.

Favorite motion effects are sorted alphabetically (see figure 8.17). To keep the same shortcuts assigned to each favorite motion, make sure you insert 01, 02, 03, and so on as part of each favorite motion's name so they stay in the correct order.

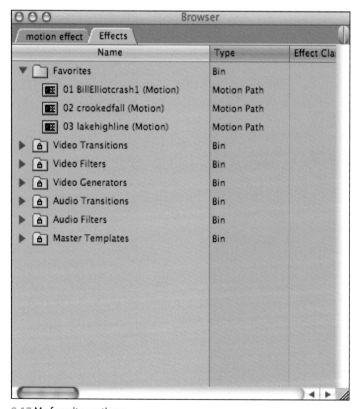

8.17 My favorite motions.

Copying and Pasting Motion Attributes

The real power of Final Cut Pro comes into play when you start copying and pasting attributes. In this section, you can learn how to copy the motion parameters from one clip to an entire group of clips.

To copy a motion parameter to other clips, follow these steps:

1. **Create a motion path for a clip in the Timeline using Bezier curves.** Create the path so the clip enters one side of the frame and exits to the other side.

2. **Right-click on the clip that you've assigned a motion path to.** Choose Copy from the contextual menu (see figure 8.18).

8.18 Copy clip using contextual menu.

3. **Assign each clip the same duration.** Right-click on each clip within the Timeline window and choose the duration from the contextual menu. The duration of each clip determines how fast the clip moves from one side of the screen to the other. If you plan on creating a composite, you want the timing to be the same for all the different clips.

4. **Highlight the rest of the clips within the Timeline and right-click on one of them.**

5. **Right-click on all the other clips within the Timeline window and choose Paste attributes from the contextual menu.** A Paste Attributes dialog appears.

6. **Click on the Basic Motion check box and press OK.** All clips now have the same motion parameters.

If you decide to change something, all you need to do is change the motion parameters for one clip and copy and paste the clip's motion attributes to all the other clips.

Working with Multiple Video Layers

To create a sense of timing, you can offset video clips by stacking them on multiple video layers. If you combine this technique with using motion parameters, you can create a sense of timing that produces a dynamic effect.

Carefully stack each clip layer on its own video layer and use a predetermined offset to create an amazing motion-effects composite. Just make sure you use the same offset each time you add another video layer to ensure that the timing stays the same (see figure 8.19).

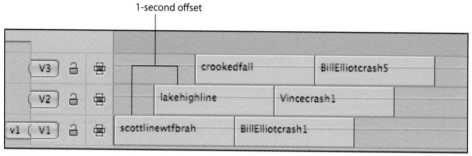

1-second offset

8.19 Clips stacked on individual video layers using an offset.

Simulating the Ken Burns Effect

Ken Burns, a famous filmmaker, perfected the use of a motion-controlled film camera for use in film documentaries. His documentaries made extensive use of still photographs, and he used an elaborate motion-control setup that allowed him to bring still photos to life. Burns did this by attaching a motion-picture camera to a mechanical arm in order to move the camera over each photograph.

You can simulate this concept in Final Cut Pro. The trick is to obtain a high-resolution picture, preferably a picture that contains a high number of megapixels.

The Ken Burns effect involves zooming in and out and moving around a photographic image within a 720x480 area in the Canvas window without losing quality of image. For best results, work with images that have a minimum of 1 megapixel. This means your camera should shoot at the equivalent of 1280x1024 or higher. The more pixels, the better.

With high-definition video now upon us (1920x1080), you need an image of 3 megapixels or more for the Ken Burns effect to be effective.

Follow these steps to create your own Ken Burns effect:

1. **Create a new DV sequence.**

2. **Import a high-resolution megapixel image into the Final Cut Pro Browser window.** Edit the clip to the timeline.

3. **Double-click on the clip within the Timeline window.** The clip's contents load into the Viewer window. Make sure your playhead indicator is parked over the first frame of the still image within the Timeline window.

4. **Click on the Motion tab within the Viewer window.** Notice that Final Cut Pro has automatically scaled the image to a value less than 100 percent in order to fit the 720x480 screen area.

5. **Change the scale parameter to a value larger than 100 percent.**

6. **Set the Canvas viewer menu to the Image+Wireframe mode.**

7. **Set the Canvas scale menu to a value less than 100 percent so you can see the entire megapixel image.** You may need to zoom out as far as 12 percent in order to see the entire image. This is your opportunity to move around within the frame (see figure 8.20). The idea here is to plot keyframes at various points to produce motion.

8. **Press Ctrl+K or click on the Add Motion Keyframe button.**

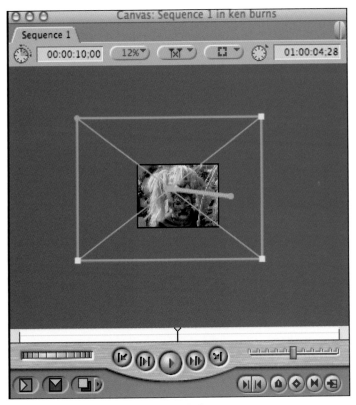

8.20 Megapixel image within Canvas window.

9. **Move the playhead to the last frame of the clip.** Drag the Image+Wireframe area to a new location. Notice a new keyframe has been created based on the position of the playhead indicator. You might also want to zoom into the image slightly. This gives the effect that you are slowly moving toward the image over time.

When you are finished back up and play the effect.

How Many Ways Can I Use Filters?

One of the key components of Final Cut Pro is the ability to use filters. Each video filter is unique, and you can combine an unlimited number of them on one clip. As a Final Cut Pro editor, it's important to understand which filters will accomplish a particular task. The standard software package ships with an excellent array of filters. Some filters are relatively complex, and others are very simple. You can also add additional filters that expand upon what ships with the software. Better yet, there is a growing list of individuals who create their own filters and offer them for free.

Tricks within the Video Filters Tab

All Final Cut Pro filters are available within the Effects tab. The Effects tab is a separate window with a tab at the top of the Browser window. Within the Effects tab, you will see a list of effects categories. The categories are broken down into folders labeled as Favorites, Video Transitions, Video Filters, Generators, and Master Templates (see figure 9.1). The Filter category contains additional folders that break down the types of filters available to you. For example, clicking the disclosure triangle for the Glow category reveals a list of all the Glow filters.

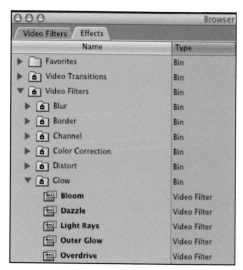

9.1 The Effects tab showing Video Filter categories.

You can apply video filters directly to clips within the Timeline window. Simply drag the filter directly from the Effects tab onto a clip within the Timeline window. Depending on the filter, you may see an instant result. There is no limit to the number of filters that you can apply to a video clip; you can stack different filters onto the same clip.

Some filters require parameter adjustments until you see anything happen. To adjust the filter parameters, double-click on a clip that contains the video filter. The Filters tab then appears at the top of the Viewer window (see figure 9.2). The Filters tab provides a list of the parameters that you can adjust for each individual filter.

Genius

You can tear off the Filters tab from the Viewer window. You can also drag the Filters tab into the Timeline window. This increases the size of the window to match the Timeline, which means you have more space for creating keyframes and adjusting parameters. When you are finished, you can right-click on the Filters tab and close it. The Filters tab automatically returns back to its default location within the Viewer window.

You can apply filters to clips using the main Effects menu or by dragging a filter from the Effects window directly to a clip. I recommend dragging filters from the Effects window instead of using the main menu.

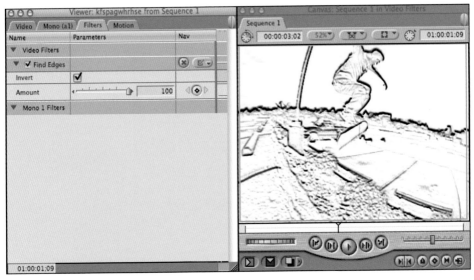

9.2 Using the Filters tab to adjust parameters.

Caution If you plan on using the main Effects menu to apply video filters, make sure a clip is highlighted within the Timeline before selecting a filter from the menu. Otherwise, the filter is applied to all video layers based on where the playhead indicator is parked. The auto-select buttons within the Timeline determine which clips will have filters applied to them when you use the main Effects drop-down menu.

You can also apply video filters to just a portion of a clip. To do this, use the Range Selection tool. Hold down your mouse button on the Final Cut Pro toolbar for a second to reveal the Range Selection tool, which is hidden underneath the Edit Selection tool (see figure 9.3).

After the Range Selection tool is activated, you can draw a specified range directly within a clip using your mouse. After you've made a range selection, simply drag a filter onto the highlighted area (see figure 9.4).

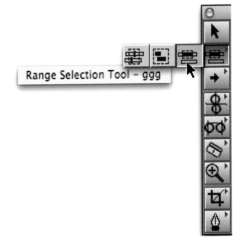

9.3 Activating the Range Selection tool.

171

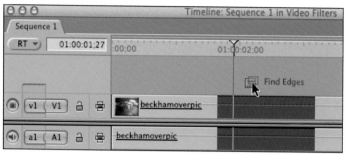

9.4 Applying a video filter to selected ranges within the Timeline.

Changing or trimming a filter area

To trim or change the location of a filter that has been applied to a clip, follow these steps:

1. **Double-click on the clip to load its contents into the Viewer window.**

2. **Click on the Filters tab at the top of the Viewer window (see figure 9.5).** Each video filter has a keyframe graph area to the right of the filter. Within the graph area, you see a start and end point for each filter.

3. **Drag the start or end point of the filter to change the filter's location within the clip.** You can also click between the start and end points to change both points together, which will slide the entire area.

Filter range start and end points

| Mark | Modify | Sequence | Effects | Tools | Window | Help |

Viewer: beckhamoverpic from Sequence 1

| Video | Mono (a1) | Filters | Motion |

Name	Parameters	Nav	00;0	01:00;
▼ Video Filters				
▼ ✔ Find Edges		⊗ ☑▾		
Invert	✔			
Amount	◀———◻ 100	◁◉▷		
▼ Mono 1 Filters				

9.5 Changing the start or end points of a video filter within a clip.

The real magic of filters comes with the ability to create keyframes. You can use keyframes to change the parameters of a filter over a specified period of time. You can add keyframes within the keyframe graph area of the Filters tab. Depending on your screen resolution, you may need to increase the size of the Viewer window in order to see the keyframe graph area of the Viewer window.

Using the Toggle Clip Keyframes feature

Since it can be cumbersome to constantly resize the Viewer window to see the keyframe graph area, you may find it easier to use the Clip Keyframes feature directly within the Timeline window.

Follow these steps to adjust a filter using the Clip Keyframes area within the Timeline window:

1. **Drag the Dazzle filter from the Effects tab to a clip within the Timeline.** The Dazzle filter is located within the Glow category.

2. **Click on the Toggle Clip Keyframes button in the lower-left corner of the Timeline menu (see figure 9.6).** The tracks within the Timeline open up to reveal a clip's keyframe area underneath each track.

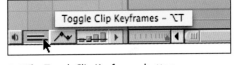

9.6 The ToggleClip Keyframes button.

3. **Expand the Clip Keyframes area to make it larger.** Expand it to about four times its original size (see figure 9.7).

4. **Right-click in the Clip Keyframes Overlay area to reveal a contextual menu (see figure 9.8).** This shows a list of filters that you can change. Filters always appear at the top of the list.

9.7 Expanding the Clip Keyframes area.

Within each filter, you see a list of filter parameters. Notice there are several parameters to choose from.

5. **Choose Amount from the contextual menu.** A green line indicator appears with the Clip Keyframes area.

6. **Drag the green line up or down to change the amount of glow within the Dazzle filter.**

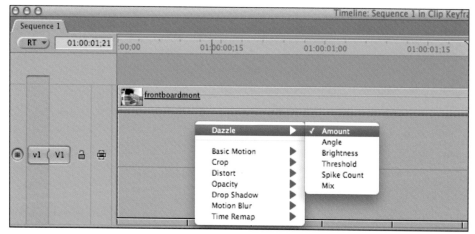

9.8 Expanding the Clip Keyframes area.

You can also add keyframes directly within the Clip Keyframes area for each individual parameter. Holding down the Option key changes the Selection tool into a Pen tool (see figure 9.9). Click on the green line while holding down the Option key to add keyframes. These keyframes allow you to change the parameter values over a specified amount of time.

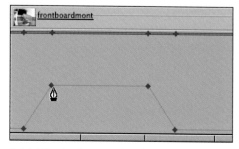

9.9 Adding keyframes using the Pen Tool.

If you want a parameter to fade up and fade down, you need a minimum of four keyframes. If you choose to adjust keyframes using the Clip Keyframe Overlay area, you have to adjust each parameter individually by right-clicking in the Overlay area and selecting the appropriate parameter.

Copying and Pasting Filter Attributes

A critical function in building effects sequences is the ability to copy and paste attributes. Using this simple concept allows you to build complex sequences that require a minimal amount of effort.

To copy and paste filter attributes, follow these steps:

1. **Right-click on any clip within the Timeline window that contains a filter and choose Copy from the contextual menu (see figure 9.10).** This copies all of the filters that have been applied to that particular clip.

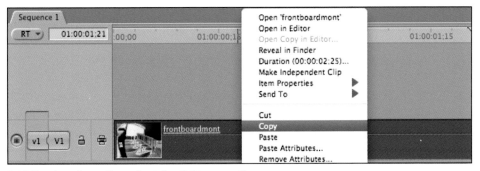

9.10 Copying clip attributes by right-clicking on a clip.

2. **Highlight a clip or a group of clips within the Timeline window.** Right-click on them and choose Paste Attributes from the contextual menu. A Paste Attributes box appears (see figure 9.11).

3. **Click the Filters check box and press OK to continue.**

You can use the Copy and Paste Attributes feature to create a rotating picture-in-picture effect with two different sides. Follow these steps to create this effect:

1. **Edit two clips directly on top of each other onto a new sequence.** Trim the clips so each of them are exactly 5 seconds in duration.

9.11 The Paste Attributes dialog box.

Caution The one drawback to using this method of pasting filters to other clips is that all of the filters are pasted. You have no ability to select individual filters to paste.

2. **Drag the Basic 3D from the Effects tab onto the clip that's on V2 in the Timeline (see figure 9.12).** You can find the Basic 3D filter in the Video Filters ➪ Perspective category.

9.12 Apply Basic 3D filter to clip on V2.

3. **Park the playhead indicator at the beginning of the clip.**

4. **Double-click on the clip to load its contents into the Viewer window.**

5. **Set the scale parameter to 50%.**

6. **Click the Insert Keyframe button for the Y axis Rotation Parameter (see figure 9.13).**

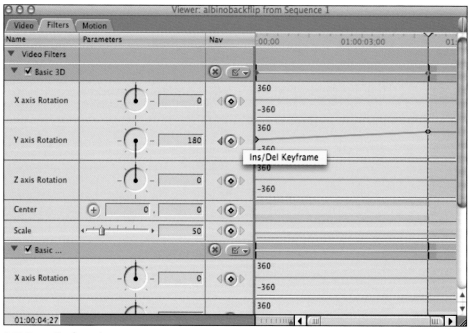

9.13 Insert Keyframe button.

7. **Place the playhead indicator at the last frame of the clip.**

8. **Set the Y axis Rotation parameter to 180.** After you add the first keyframe for any parameter, new keyframes are automatically created based on the location of the playhead indicator any time you readjust a parameter.

9. **Play the sequence.** The clip on V2 should spin on its y axis over the top of the background
   video, which is on V1.

10. **Copy and paste the filter attributes from the clip on V2 to the clip on V1.** Both clips now
    have the same exact filter attributes.

11. **Trim back the duration of the top clip on V2 halfway, which is exactly 2.5 seconds (see
    figure 9.14).** Drag the clip back halfway to reveal the V1 clip underneath it. You now have a
    rotating clip with different front and back sides (see figure 9.15).

9.14 Trimming back the V2 layer.

9.15 Picture-in-picture effect with two different sides.

Saving and Configuring Your Favorite Filters

The ability to store favorite filters is another critical component to building effects. The basic concept is to store individual filters that you create in order to build other complex effects. Let's say
you decide that you really like the effect that you've just built of the rotating picture-in-picture

effect. Instead of having to copy and paste filter attributes, you can save the filter as a favorite that you can use repeatedly. Better yet, you can map the filter to a shortcut key on your keyboard.

To save a favorite filter, follow these steps:

1. **Double-click on the clip that contains the Basic 3D effect.** The clip's contents load into the Viewer window.

2. **Click on the Filters tab within the Viewer window.**

3. **Highlight the Basic 3D effect inside the Filters window.**

4. **Navigate to the Effects menu ➪ Make Favorite Effect.** This places the Basic 3D filter into the favorite's folder located within the Effects tab inside the Browser window.

Anytime you need your favorite effect, you can access it from the Effects window under the favorite's folder.

Genius

As you build a list of favorite effects, change the name of each effect so it starts with a number 01, 02, and so on. This forces Final Cut Pro to sort the effects numerically.

Building filter packs

If you save a favorite video effect that has multiple filters, a filter pack is stored inside the Favorites folder within the Effects tab (see figure 9.16). A filter pack works just like a favorite effect, except it contains multiple filters all within one folder. To apply a filter pack, drag the folder onto a clip or a group of clips. Unfortunately, you cannot map filter packs to buttons or keys.

Mapping favorite effects to shortcut keys or buttons

You can map your favorite effects directly to a shortcut key or a button. Doing this will really improve your speed and efficiency when it comes to building effects.

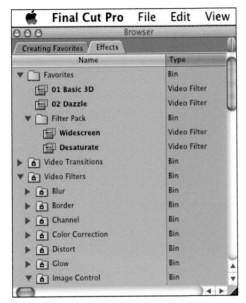

9.16 Effect favorites.

To map a favorite filter to a shortcut key, follow these steps:

1. **Navigate to the Tools menu ⇨ Keyboard Layout ⇨ Customize.**

2. **In the upper-right corner of the Keyboard Layout, type the words** video filter **inside the search box.** Do not press the Return key, otherwise nothing will happen. A list of video filter favorite buttons appears within the Keyboard Layout. You can map up to nine different video filter favorites to buttons or keys.

3. **Drag the Video Filter Favorite #1 button into one of the button wells or onto one of the keys within the Keyboard Layout (see figure 9.17).** You can find button wells in all the major Final Cut Pro interface windows.

9.17 Button well within the Canvas window.

You can remove a button from a button well by dragging it outside of the well. When using the video favorite buttons to add effects, you only need to place your playhead indicator over a particular clip and press the button. That's it! The effect automatically applies to any video layer that the playhead indicator is parked over.

Toggling the Auto Select function

When applying a video effect or filter to a clip, it is not always necessary to select a clip in the Timeline. You can use the Auto Select buttons within the Final Cut Pro Timeline to tell Final Cut Pro which video layers will be affected when you apply a video effect from any of the Final Cut Pro menus. This includes effects that are applied from using a shortcut key. The trick is that you must have the playhead indicator parked over the clips that you want affected.

The default keyboard shortcut to manage the Auto Selects is ⌘+*track number*. For example, ⌘+2 toggles the Auto Select for V2 (see figure 9.18).

Caution Make sure you toggle the correct Auto Select buttons on or off before adding a favorite effect that has been mapped to a shortcut key. The default setting is for all the Auto Select icons to be turned on.

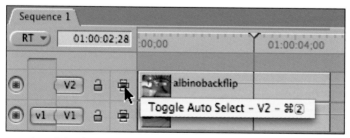

9.18 Auto Select button.

Genius

To do the same thing using a favorite effect, follow these steps:

1. **Copy two clips to a new sequence and stack them directly on top of each other.**

2. **Place the playhead indicator over the clips and press the favorite effect button.**

3. **Drag the top clip on V2 back halfway to reveal the side of the clip below it.**

If you stop and think about this, the previous exercise required ten steps. Now you can do it in three!

Why the order of stacked filters is important

Final Cut Pro processes filters from top to bottom. Whatever filter you apply first is processed first. To demonstrate this, if you go back to the rotating picture-in-picture exercise, you'll notice that when the picture-in-picture flips around on its y axis, the video image on the back side is reversed.

To fix this, you need to apply a Flop filter to the back side of the image. Both clips are stacked directly on top of each other, V2 on the front and V1 on the back. You can find the Flop filter in the Perspective category of the Video Filters category. The Flop filter does exactly what it says: It flops the image so the contents are reversed. If a person in the frame was right-handed, they would now be left-handed. The one real caveat is if someone in the clip has a shirt with a logo or words across it. Flopping an image like that would be an obvious blunder because the words would appear backward.

Occasionally you can still get away with flopping images and no one will notice, but sometimes applying the Flop filter isn't enough to solve the problem. In this case, applying a Flop filter to the clip would also flop the animation parameters of the rotating picture-in-picture effect (see figure 9.19). You need to take an additional step to change how the effects are processed.

9.19 Filters arranged in the wrong order produce an unacceptable result.

To adjust the processing order of filters within a clip follow these steps:

1. **Double-click on a clip within the Timeline that contains multiple filters.** In this example, it would be the clip on V1. This loads the clip's contents into the Viewer window.

2. **Within the Viewer window, click on the Filters tab.** This shows the filters that have been applied to that particular clip.

3. **Drag the Flop filter above the Basic 3D filter (see figure 9.20).** This changes the processing order so Final Cut Pro processes the Flop filter first.

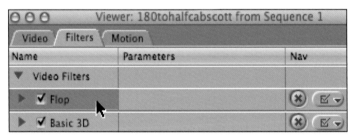

9.20 Rearranging the order of filters.

Duplicating Video Layers

Remember that when you build an effect's composites, it's all about how the video layers are stacked. Let's say you want to create a 3D title that has the appearance of tinted transparent glass. You can easily achieve this effect by stacking a couple of layers on top of each other.

An effect like this also requires the use of composite modes. It is a basic concept to composite a video layer inside a title. By duplicating layers, you can have separate control of what's inside the text, as well as control the look of the background. Since the video inside the text and the background video are exactly the same, it gives the illusion that the characters of the title are made of transparent glass (see figure 9.21). To review how composite modes work within Final Cut Pro, refer to Chapter 7.

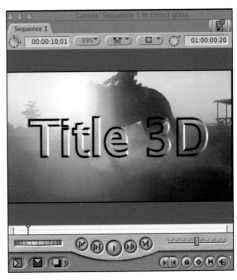

9.21 Effects composite in the Canvas window.

You can duplicate a clip directly above itself in the Timeline by clicking Option+Shift and dragging the clip up a layer. If you haven't created an additional video track, Final Cut Pro automatically creates a new one for you. Also, if your clip has audio attached to it, remember to lock the clip's audio track so you don't end up with two duplicate audio tracks.

Follow these steps to create a title with a tinted glass effect:

1. **Edit a video clip to an empty Timeline.** This will be the background video.

2. **Build a title using the Title 3D title tool and place it directly above the clip on V2.** Make the title fairly large with a point size of 132 or higher. Make the title completely white with no edges or drop shadows.

3. **Create a duplicate title directly above itself onto V3.** Click Option+Shift and drag the title from V2 to V3. You should now have two identical titles directly on top of each other (see figure 9.22).

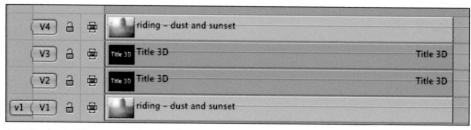

9.22 Duplicate titles on top of each other.

4. **Create a duplicate of the clip on V1 onto V4.** Click Option+Shift and drag V1 to V4.

5. **Right-click on the clip that's on V4 and choose the contextual menu ⇨ Composite Mode ⇨ Travel Matte–Alpha.** The text disappears, but don't worry. The title disappeared because the top and bottom video layers have the same video content.

Genius

You can use the Superimpose feature to automatically place a title directly above another clip within the Final Cut Pro Timeline. The keyboard shortcut for Superimpose is F12.

Caution

Make sure you have disabled the Exposé feature within Mac OS X, or the Superimpose feature will not work correctly. You can refer to Chapter 1 on how to do this.

6. **Double-click on the title that's on V2.** The clip's contents load into the Viewer window.

7. **Click on the Controls tab within the Viewer window.** Select Click for Options. This relaunches the Boris Title 3D interface window.

8. **Change the title by adding a beveled edge on the outside edge of the text.** For more information on how to add an edge with the Title 3D title tool, refer to Chapter 6.

You should now have a title that appears to be like transparent glass.

Genius

You can apply filters to either V4 or V1 to affect what's inside the text vs. what's inside the background. V4 is the video inside the text, and V1 is the background video. For example, you could change the background video to black and white by applying a Desaturate filter to V1 without affecting what's inside the text.

Color Correction

Final Cut Pro provides a fairly robust color correction tool in the 3-Way Color Corrector filter. For most of us, the 3-Way Color Corrector will suffice in correcting all types of footage. That being said, the current version of Final Cut Studio also ships with a separate application called Color. Color is a full-blown color-correction program that includes its own built-in effects interface. For this book, I focus on using the 3-Way Color Corrector directly within Final Cut Pro.

Adjusting blacks, mid, and white values

The 3-Way Color Corrector filter provides individual color controls for highlights, shadows, and the midranges of the color spectrum. This means that you can adjust the brighter areas of an image without affecting the darker parts of an image. More importantly, you can also tell the color corrector to correct a specific range of colors. You can find the 3-Way Color Corrector within the Video Filters ➪ Color Correction category (see figure 9.23).

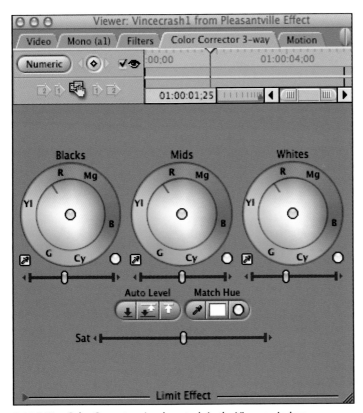

9.23 3-Way Color Corrector visual controls in the Viewer window.

Adjusting playhead sync for color-correcting multiple clips

If you are serious about using the color correction tools within Final Cut Pro, it is sometimes necessary to color-correct every shot within a sequence. It can become cumbersome applying the 3-Way Color Corrector to every single clip and then double-clicking on each clip in order to adjust the settings.

An easier way to apply the 3-Way Color Corrector filter to every clip within your sequence is to simply highlight the entire Final Cut Pro sequence and drag the 3-Way Color Corrector filter to all the selected clips. However, you still need to double-click on each clip that you wish to adjust in order to get access to the 3-Way Color Correction controls. If you have hundreds of clips within your sequence, this is still quite time-consuming.

Fortunately, there is a fantastic feature that forces Final Cut Pro to automatically open each clip within the Viewer window as you place the playhead indicator over individual clips. This means that you only need to park over the clip that you want to color-correct, and the 3-Way Color Corrector controls become instantly available. This dramatically lessens the amount of time you will spend on color-correcting an entire project.

Activate this special function by selecting Open in the Playhead Sync drop-down menu (see figure 9.24). The Playhead Sync menu is located at the top center of the Viewer and Canvas windows. Both menus work together, so it doesn't matter which one you turn on. Once the Playhead Sync menu is set to Open, Final Cut Pro automatically opens each clip directly into the Viewer window when you place the playhead indicator over individual clips.

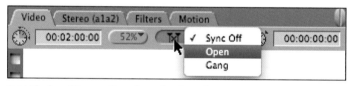

9.24 Playhead Sync options from the drop-down menu.

Pleasantville effect

You can use the 3-Way Color Corrector to produce the Pleasantville effect (see figure 9.25). The term *Pleasantville effect* is derived from the Hollywood movie *Pleasantville,* where everything is black and white except for certain objects or people. Believe it or not, this is a relatively easy effect to produce. The only catch is that you need to find a particular color that only pertains to one object within the video frame. For example, if you had a person with a red shirt and nothing else within the frame contained red, this would work well for building the Pleasantville effect.

To create the Pleasantville effect using the 3-Way Color Corrector, follow these steps:

1. **Edit a clip to an empty Timeline.** Again, pick your clip carefully based on finding something that has a particular color that is unique to the rest of the video image.

2. **Drag the 3-Way Color Corrector filter from the Effects window onto the clip within the Timeline.**

3. **Double-click on the clip within the Timeline window.** The clip's contents load into the Viewer window.

4. **Within the Viewer window, click on the 3-Way Color Corrector tab.** The color-correction controls for the 3-Way Color Corrector appear.

5. **Click on the disclosure triangle located at the bottom-left corner to reveal the Limit Effect parameters.**

6. **Use the eyedropper to pick a unique color from the video image within the Canvas window.** Again, you want to pick a color for an object that isn't anywhere else in the frame.

7. **Within the Canvas window, turn off the blue check boxes for limit Sat and limit Luma.**

8. **Expand the color range area by pulling apart the pins at the top of the color range bar.** It's sort of a guessing game on how much color to include. Make the range larger until you're confident you've selected enough of the color. In this example, the range for the color red has been expanded.

9. **Slide the Sat (saturation) slider all the way to the left.** The rest of image should turn black and white without affecting the color that you've selected.

10. **Click on the Invert Selection button.** That's it! You should now have something that resembles the Pleasantville effect.

You can use the Softening slider to help blend the edges of the color that you've selected. You can also adjust the color slightly. Worst-case scenario, just start over again by picking a different color, or more of the color with the eyedropper.

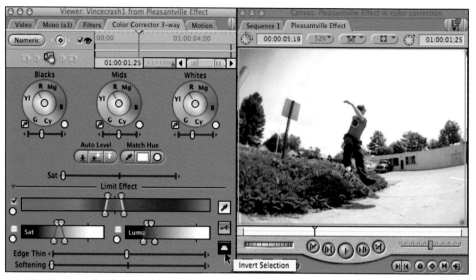

9.25 The Pleasantville effect.

Understanding Nesting

Nesting allows Final Cut Pro to collapse tracks so they can be used together and treated as a group instead of individual layers. The beautiful thing about nesting is that you still have access to the individual layers. If you need to go back and change something, you still have that option.

A perfect example of why you might want to nest video layers would be if you wanted to apply a special-effect treatment to an entire sequence. This could be something simple like applying a Desaturation filter to your entire sequence in order to make it black and white. Or you could apply a 16x9 mask to an entire sequence to give it a letterboxed look.

You can also use nesting to collapse a bunch of video layers taking up too much space. Nothing is more frustrating than if you have a bunch of video layers at the beginning of your sequence for an opening effects sequence. It's then frustrating to edit the rest of the content, because you have many video tracks taking up the Timeline area. You can nest those complicated effects so they only take up one track, making it much easier to edit the rest of the show.

To create a nested clip, do the following:

1. **Highlight the clips within a sequence that you want to nest together.**

2. **Navigate to the Sequence menu ⇨ Nest Items.** All the selected video tracks become a single nested clip.

Remember the Moving Filmstrip effect from Chapter 8? You can use nesting to collapse those layers into a single nested layer (see figure 9.26), which you can reopen to access the individual layers or you can treat it as a single clip element. Double-clicking on a nested clip opens the clip to reveal the nested contents. An additional sequence tab opens up within the Timeline window to indicate that you are working within the nest. To get back outside a nested clip, just click back onto the original sequence tab.

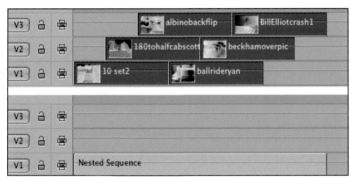

9.26 Example of nesting clips together.

If you drag a nested clip into the Viewer window you can adjust the nested clip as a whole. For example, if you nest the Moving Filmstrip effect from Chapter 8, you can adjust the Filmstrip effect as a whole. To do this, drag the nested clip into the Viewer window. By using the controls within the Motion tab, you can now add a drop shadow, reposition, or rotate the entire filmstrip (see figure 9.27).

Final Cut Pro also retains any transparent layers underneath the original layers as part of the nested clip. All the pieces inside the filmstrip stay intact. Better yet, double-click on the nested clip to open the nest and readjust each of clips within the filmstrip individually.

189

9.27 Modifying a nested clip within the Viewer window.

When you import a .psd file, Final Cut Pro automatically treats the file as a nested sequence. Each layer within the nest represents an individual Photoshop layer (see figure 9.28). This means that you can adjust the individual layers within the nest.

Caution While Final Cut Pro recognizes Photoshop layers within a .psd file, it does not recognize Photoshop effects layers such as glows, beveled edges, and drop shadows. Therefore, if you plan on using Photoshop effects layers, you need to convert them to traditional Photoshop layers in order for Final Cut Pro to see them. Unless you need access to the individual .psd layers within Final Cut Pro, I recommend that you save the your file as .png instead of using a .psd file.

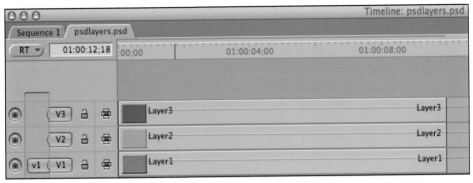

9.28 Modifying a nested clip within the Viewer window.

Chroma Keying

Chroma keying (also known as *blue* or *green screen* in Hollywood) can be a tricky process. Using a chroma key involves removing one particular color of the color spectrum on a video layer, thereby revealing the background video layer underneath it. For the most part, chroma keys are done on a blue or green background. Blue produces the best results, with green being a close second. Since blue occupies more wavelength than any other color, it also produces the cleanest-looking chroma key. That's why all major television stations use a blue background when doing the weather forecast.

The one drawback of using blue is that it's also the most popular color, meaning a lot of individuals wear the color blue whether it's blue jeans or blue within their shirt. So green is the next best choice, providing an adequate wavelength.

Professionals will tell you that the key to producing a good chroma key is making sure the green screen or blue screen is well-lit. Fortunately, Final Cut Pro has some tools in place to produce an excellent chroma key, even if your lighting conditions aren't ideal. You can also use Motion or Color to produce a chroma key effect, which are two separate applications that come bundled with Final Cut Studio.

Genius

If you do not have an indoor studio with perfect lighting conditions, there are companies that produce portable green screens that you can use indoors or outdoors. An advantage of working outdoors is that natural sunlight provides excellent lighting conditions. Just make sure your subject stands at least 5 feet from the front of the screen so she doesn't leave any shadows on the chroma key background.

Follow these steps to produce a chroma key effect:

1. **Place your background clip on V1.**

2. **Place the Chroma Key subject on V2, meaning your talent who's in front of a green screen.**

3. **Place the Chroma Keyer filter into V2.** The Chroma Keyer filter is located within the Video Filters ⇨ Key category within the Effects window.

4. **Double-click on the clip that's on V2.** This loads the clip's contents into the Viewer window.

5. **Click on the Chroma Keyer tab within the Viewer window.** This gives you access to the Chroma Keyer controls.

6. **Click on the eyedropper and then click on a green area of the clip within the Canvas window.** For best results, I recommend expanding the color range area to incorporate more green by dragging the top two pins at the top of the color range bar (see figure 9.29). I also recommend that you uncheck the Sat and Luma controls.

You will also find Edge Thin and Softening controls at the bottom of the Chroma Keyer window. For more advanced users, click on the Numeric button located in the upper-left corner of the window to activate chroma key controls that mirror the visual interface controls.

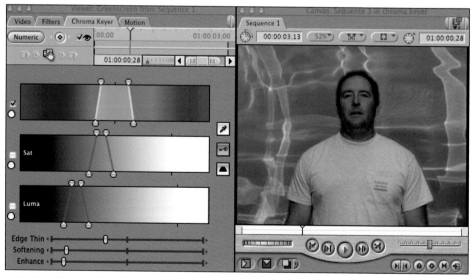

9.29 Using Chroma Keyer filter to remove green background from a clip.

Rendering Shapes

In the bottom right corner of the Viewer window is an icon that looks like the letter A. This is the Generator menu. Within the Generator menu, there are several categories to choose from, including a category called Shapes. At first, these shapes might seem a bit boring. Believe it or not, these basic shapes can play a big role in effects compositing. Start with the concept of being able to blur out a person's face or a license plate on a car.

Using shapes as masks

To track and blur out an object or a person's face, follow these steps:

1. **Edit a video clip of a person who you want to blur out a section of their face on an empty Timeline.**

2. **Navigate to the Generator menu and choose the Shapes menu ➪ Circle (see figure 9.30).** A white circle appears within the Viewer window.

3. **Edit the white circle directly above the video clip that you placed onto V1.**

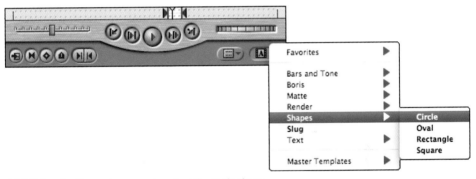

9.30 Using the Generator menu to select the circle shape.

Genius

Press the F12 key to automatically superimpose a clip above another clip within the Timeline. If you have your white circle in the Viewer window, you can just press F12 and the duration automatically matches the clip the below it.

4. **Make an exact copy of V1 onto V3 by clicking Option+Shift and dragging V1 to V3.** If don't have a V3 track, don't worry — Final Cut Pro creates one for you automatically. If your clip has audio, you may want to lock the audio track before moving it up to V3. Otherwise

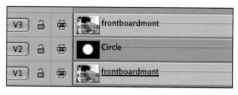

9.31 Timeline window showing three tracks with a circle shape on V2.

you end up with duplicate audio tracks. Before moving onto the next step, make sure your sequence has a white circle sandwiched between V1 and V3 (see figure 9.31).

5. **Apply a Gaussian Blur filter to V3.** Adjust the Blur filter by double-clicking on the V3 clip. The contents load into the Viewer window. You see the Filter tab at the top of the Viewer window, where you can adjust the filter.

6. **Right-click on V3 to composite V3 into V2 using the contextual menu composite mode ⇨ Travel Matte – Luma.** This places the blurred-out video, which is on V3, inside the area of the circle.

You should now have a circle with the blurry part of the video image inside the circle. The trick is to animate the circle to match the location of the person's face. This is done by plotting keyframes, beginning with the first frame of the video.

Follow these steps to track an object by manually creating keyframes:

1. **Double-click on the circle which is on V2.** Park the playhead indicator on the first frame of the video clip.

2. **Enter into Image+Wireframe mode within the Canvas window.** You can find the Image+Wireframe mode within the upper-right corner of the Canvas window from the View drop-down menu.

3. **Click on the Add Motion Keyframe button in the right corner of the Canvas window.** The Add Motion Keyframe button looks like a small diamond. Pressing this button places keyframes for all the motion parameters. The crosshairs for the Image+Wireframe area turn green, indicating that keyframes have been set for that location.

4. **Move the playhead indicator forward a bit and adjust the Image+Wireframe area to cover up the person's face (see figure 9.32).** Each time you move the playhead indicator forward, you need to adjust the Image+Wireframe area of the circle to match the person's face. You can change position, or scale the wireframe as needed in order to track the person's face. It is up to you to decide how many keyframes are necessary to get the job done.

9.32 Using Image+Wireframe mode to plot keyframes for circle shape.

Working with Boris vector shapes

There is another way to create shapes within Final Cut Pro. Within the Generator menu, you can find Boris ⇨ Vector Shape. The vector shapes are different, because they come prebuilt on a transparent background. Solid shapes are sometimes important for elements that you need to mask out. For example, you might need a black shape to mask out a person's face.

Even though the default background color for vector shapes appears to be black, the background is actually transparent. You can test this by setting the View drop-down window to either Checkerboard 1 or Checkerboard 2 (see figure 9.33). Doing so should reveal a checkerboard background, which indicates the image contains an alpha channel.

Vector shapes are excellent for creating masks and highlighting areas of a video image. Clicking on the Controls tab within the Viewer window provides a wealth of controls that allow for independent control of the shape's color, border, and shadow.

Genius

When using vector shapes, it is best to edit a generic vector shape to the Timeline first and then double-click on the vector shape. This reloads the clip into the Viewer window. As long as the playhead indicator is parked over the vector shape within the sequence, you can see changes that you make to the vector shape within the Canvas window.

To composite a video image inside a vector shape, right-click on a top video layer directly above the shape and use the contextual menu composite mode ⇨ Travel Matte – Alpha.

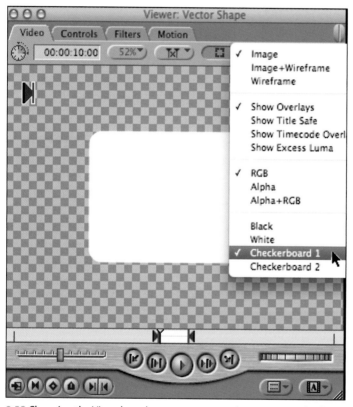

9.33 Changing the View drop-down menu to reveal a transparent background.

Rendering backgrounds

Within the Generator menu, you can render a variety of different backgrounds or particles under the Render menu. There are all sorts of backgrounds that you can create, including clouds, gradients, membranes, and lens flares. You should experiment with each of them to see how they all work. Better yet, each background has parameters that can be keyframed. For example, you could create a membrane pattern that changes from one color to another color over a specified amount of time.

When you create keyframes for colors, Final Cut Pro goes around the color wheel when going from one keyframe to another. This means that if you were to create one keyframe at the beginning of a clip parameter to be red and the last keyframe to be blue, Final Cut Pro moves through colors around the color wheel starting at red to reach blue. Which direction does Final Cut Pro choose when changing from one color to another? You can change the direction of its path around the color wheel by clicking on the Hue Direction Control button (see figure 9.34). For example, if you want to create a lens flare that changes color over time, you could control the direction of its color change as it progresses around the color wheel by clicking on this button.

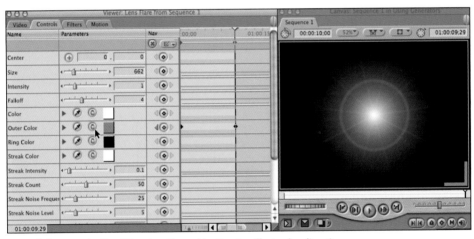

9.34 Clicking on the Hue Direction Control button to affect color direction.

Working with Master Templates

Final Cut Studio ships with a software product called Motion. Within Motion, you can create motion graphic templates. These templates show up automatically in the Generator menu under the Master Templates menu category. Each template contains a different design that you can alter in terms of changing the text, text size, text position, and video content.

Final Cut Pro supplies an excellent set of prebuilt Master Templates that you can use. After you've mastered the prebuilt templates, you can build new ones using Motion. You can adjust the parameters for each individual template by clicking on the Controls tab within the Viewer window. Again, it is best to edit your template to the Timeline first and then double-click on the template within the Timeline to reopen it into the Viewer window.

Some of the Master Templates contain something called a clip well. A clip well looks like a gray box with a question mark inside it. By dropping a clip inside a clip well, you change the contents of the Master Template (see figure 9.35). You can drag a graphic or a clip directly from the Browser window into any clip well.

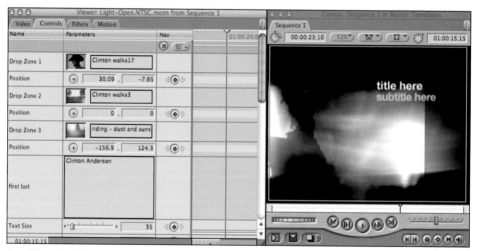

9.35 Changing Master Template in the Viewer window.

Caution

The original template themes from Final Cut Pro are locked. When changing or updating a template within Motion, you need to create a new theme before you can save the template.

You can also edit a Master Template directly in Motion by right-clicking on the clip within the Final Cut Pro sequence and choosing Open in Editor from the contextual menu. This automatically opens the template back into Motion. Remember, Motion is a separate application that ships with Final Cut Studio. You can then make changes to the design and resave it as another Master Template.

To save a Motion Project as a template, navigate to File ⇨ Save as Template. Then give the template a new name and specify a category for one of the themes (see figure 9.36).

9.36 Saving a new template within Motion.

The video production industry is experiencing a dramatic shift from tape-based formats to tapeless technologies. Because of this, it's no longer as simple as pressing Play and Record on a tape machine to make a copy of your Final Cut Pro product. The industry is rapidly adopting various digital multimedia formats as a way of outputting your final product. Therefore, it is absolutely essential to understand the various output options when working with Final Cut Pro. You don't want to export poor-quality copies of your final sequence.

Final Cut Pro Sequence Settings

In Final Cut Pro, you can mix resolutions and frame rates in the same sequence. Believe it or not, this is becoming quite common. There are a myriad of different HD (High Definition) and SD (Standard Definition) formats, and it is common to receive media from a variety of different formats. What is an editor supposed to do? Your best bet is to mix everything to the highest format available.

If your final output is high definition, you want the best quality when converting clips that are in standard definition. Fortunately, Final Cut Pro does this for you automatically. However, you need to specify some settings on how to handle these types of situations.

Let's start with the adjusting the general video processing functions.

1. **Highlight your sequence in the Browser window and right-click it to choose Settings from the contextual menu.** The Sequence Settings dialog appears.

2. **Click the Render all YUV material in high-precision YUV radio button (see figure 10.1).**

3. **Set the Motion Filtering Quality sequence setting to Best to optimize scaling from standard definition to high definition.** This setting also optimizes motion effects renders: scaling, cropping, and rotation.

Caution Because these settings increase the amount of computer processing, I recommend that you make these changes when you are finished with your sequence.

Next, you want to take a look at the Render Control options. I recommend changing the Master Templates and Motion Projects setting to Best (see figure 10.2). I also recommend turning on the Always Use Best Quality When Rendering Movies option. Many Final Cut Pro users forget to adjust these settings before they output their final sequence.

Because tape-based technologies are rapidly becoming obsolete, let's focus on outputting your final sequence to a multimedia format. This probably means that you are either creating a DVD or exporting a multimedia file for the Web.

By changing your sequence settings to a more robust codec, you increase the file size and the depth of the video in terms of quality and color space. The best example of this is switching your sequence to an uncompressed codec, such as 10-bit uncompressed, or the animation codec. After changing the sequence settings to one of these higher-quality codecs, you see an increase in color depth and clarity in the Canvas window.

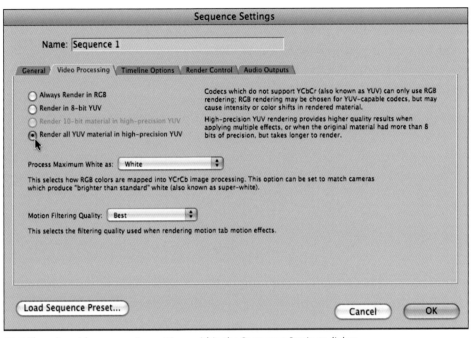

10.1 Changing video processing settings within the Sequence Settings dialog.

10.2 Render Control settings within the Sequence Settings dialog.

By changing your sequence settings to a better codec, you may notice a dramatic difference in the quality of graphics and titles. If you've noticed that titles from LiveType don't seem to look as good as they did in LiveType, it's because LiveType works with the Animation codec and most Final Cut Pro users are working with a DV codec. Once you change your sequence settings to the Animation codec, your titles from LiveType will look much better.

Caution It's best to change your sequence settings when you are completely finished. Otherwise, you may encounter a red render bar across your entire sequence. It would be quite frustrating to edit without being able to see your video in real-time. Don't worry; you can always change it back if you need to continue editing.

Follow these steps to adjust your sequence settings:

1. **Right-click your finished sequence within the Browser window and choose Settings from the contextual menu.** The Sequence Settings dialog appears.

2. **Within the Sequence Settings dialog, change the compressor settings to a higher-quality codec.** If you're not sure which codec to choose, you can always use the Animation codec (see figure 10.3).

10.3 The Compression menu in the Sequence Settings dialog.

3. **Right-click your sequence in the Browser window and select Export ⇨ QuickTime Movie from the contextual menu.** A Save dialog appears. Give the file a name and click the Save button.

Caution By changing your sequence settings to the highest-quality codec possible, you are also dramatically increasing the size. The 10-bit uncompressed codec requires over seven times more storage capacity than the DV/DVCPRO codec.

In figure 10.4, you can see the same clip compressed two different ways. Take a look at the difference in the data rate.

	Name	▲	Data Rate	Vid Rate	Duration	Out	Media Start	Media End	Tracks
	Extreme Sports	Effects							
	standard dv clip		3.5 MB/sec	29.97 fps	00:00:02:21	Not Set	00:00:00:00	00:00:02:20	1V, 1A
	10 bit codec clip		26.5 MB/sec	29.97 fps	00:00:02:21	Not Set	01:00:00:00	01:00:02:20	1V, 2A

Browser

10.4 The data rate for 10-bit uncompressed media.

Caution If you plan on sending your QuickTime movie file to another computer, make sure you choose a codec that is available on the computer you are sending the file to. In most cases, the Animation codec is readily available on most recent PCs. This means that you can transmit a high-quality movie file to another computer and ensure that it will play.

Working with Anamorphic 16x9 Media

Working with 16x9 media can be quite confusing. Most of the confusion stems from SD 16x9 images. I'm talking about cameras that shoot in 16x9 (standard definition) within a 4x3 frame. This leads to a video image that is stretched and tall when viewed directly from the camera. Fortunately, Final Cut Pro handles this type of media fairly well.

The newest HD formats are already formatted as 16x9, so you don't have the problem of whether video is anamorphic or not.

To keep things simple, Final Cut Pro automatically resizes any media that is tagged as being anamorphic as long as you are working within a standard DV/DVCPRO sequence. When you shoot 16x9 with a DV camera, it is automatically tagged as anamorphic. Final Cut Pro reads this information, and it knows to resize the video image to fit a standard 4x3 picture. The key, believe it or not, is to let Final Cut Pro do all the reformatting for you.

Caution You may run into a situation where you capture something from a non-DV source that contains anamorphic media. In this case, the anamorphic tag is not present. You need to manually check the anamorphic check box for each clip.

You can verify whether a clip is tagged as anamorphic by right-clicking the clip within the Browser window and selecting Item Properties ⇨ Format from the contextual menu. The Item Properties dialog appears. You see an Anamorphic setting that is either checked or unchecked (see figure 10.5).

Item Properties: riding – dust and sunset		
	Clip	V1
Name	riding – dust and sunset	riding – dust and sunset
Type	Clip	
Creator	Final Cut Pro	Final Cut Pro
Source	Macintosh HD:Users:Shared:CLASS MEDIA	Macintosh HD:Users:Sha
Offline		
Size	34.4 MB	34.4 MB
Last Modified	Sat, Apr 23, 2005, 2:37 PM	Sat, Apr 23, 2005, 2:37
Tracks	1V	
Vid Rate	29.97 fps	29.97 fps
Frame Size	720 x 480	720 x 480
Compressor	DV/DVCPRO – NTSC	DV/DVCPRO – NTSC
Data Rate	3.4 MB/sec	3.4 MB/sec
Pixel Aspect	NTSC – CCIR 601	NTSC – CCIR 601
Anamorphic	✔	✔
Gamma Level		
Field Dominance	Lower (Even)	Lower (Even)
SmoothCam	--	
Alpha	None/Ignore	None/Ignore
Reverse Alpha		
Composite	Normal	Normal
Audio		
Aud Rate		

[Cancel]   [OK]

10.5 The Anamorphic setting for a clip in the Item Properties dialog.

Leaving the Anamorphic check box selected automatically reformats anamorphic media to fit within a 4x3 frame. Without the Anamorphic setting turned on, the clip in figure 10.6 would be tall and stretched within the 4x3 frame (see figure 10.6).

10.6 A stretched clip.

Working with QuickTime

QuickTime is more than a media player. The Apple Developer Connection page (http://developer. apple.com/quicktime/) describes QuickTime as a "multimedia software architecture." Final Cut Studio uses this architecture for its applications. The Developer Connection site also states that "QuickTime also provides file format converters for more than 250 common image, video, and audio file formats." In addition to these formats, QuickTime includes a plug-in architecture that allows developers to create code for formats that Apple doesn't support.

For example, Flip4Mac (www.flip4mac.com/wmv.htm) sells plug-ins that allow you to view, edit, convert, and encode Windows Media Video (WMV) within QuickTime. Because Final Cut Studio uses the QuickTime architecture, the high-end plug-in also adds 2-pass encoding for WMV files to Compressor.

These conversion options are only available if you have a QuickTime Pro license. Fortunately, all users of Final Cut Studio automatically have QuickTime Pro installed on their computers, and so no additional action is needed.

With the popularity of digital video systems, some users are playing back their QuickTime movies using the Apple QuickTime player for video for presentations.

Make sure you enable the high-quality video setting in QuickTime. You can find this setting by selecting QuickTime Player ➪ Preferences ➪ General (see figure 10.7). This setting affects files using the DV codec. The default setting has the high-quality playback option turned off. Once you've enabled the setting, you need to relaunch QuickTime. If you perform any updates, you need to reenable the setting. The same setting is available for QuickTime player for PCs. Many users are unaware of this setting and end up presenting their movie without using the highest-quality video setting.

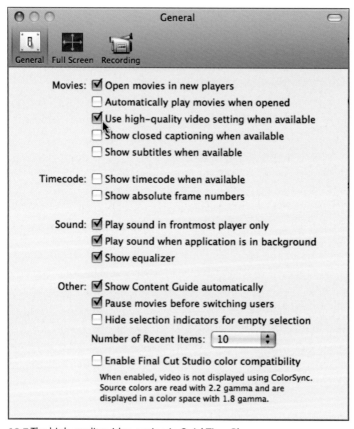

10.7 The high-quality video setting in QuickTime Player.

Exporting for DVD Production

DVDs that play in your standard DVD player contain physical data on the disk in the format of MPEG-2 compression. HD Blu-Ray disks support MPEG-2 compression along with some other codecs. The term *codec* stands for compression/decompression. It simply refers to how data is compressed and then decompressed.

MPEG-2 compression implements something called GOP (Group of Pictures), which is a collection of frames designed to play back video. There are three types of frames: I-frames, P-frames, and B-frames. Table 10.1 discusses these frames and their compression types.

Table 10.1 GOP Structure for MPEG-2

Type of Frame	Compression Type
I-Frame	Compressed independently for the highest-quality image.
P-Frame	Predictive (uses information from previous I and P frames) providing less image quality.
B-Frame	Uses information from I and P frames that precede and follow it, thus providing the lowest amount of quality.

Bottom line, the more I-Frames that you have, the better quality the DVD. I-Frames take up the most space, as they are full frames. B-Frames offer the lowest amount of quality. If you have too many B-Frames in an MPEG-2 file, a scene with a lot of motion looks very bad. Don't worry; your DVD authoring program handles all the encoding for you.

Right out of the box, you can use either iDVD or DVD Studio Pro to actually create your physical DVD disk. iDVD is one of the iLife applications that ship with every Mac. It is incredibly easy to use and straightforward when it comes time to produce your DVD.

Caution

As cool and easy as iDVD is to use, it has some limitations. The biggest is that you have no control over the MPEG-2 compression settings. It uses a 1-pass setting when compressing a movie. This means that the video quality of your project may suffer as a result of using iDVD. If you are concerned with the quality of your video, it is best to learn Apple Compressor in combination with DVD Studio Pro.

The recent version of Final Cut Pro does not provide for an MPEG-2 export option. This option has been moved over into Apple Compressor. You need to send your final sequence into Apple Compressor to produce an MPEG-2 file.

Genius

Regardless of whether you are preparing a sequence for iDVD or DVD Studio Pro, you should output your sequence using the highest-quality setting possible. I recommend staying away from the standard DV-DVCPRO codec, as this codec processes video within a smaller color space.

Using Apple Compressor

Even though DVD Studio Pro provides control for compressing your video, I recommend that you preprocess your video through Apple Compressor. Apple Compressor can quickly become one of the most important applications in Final Cut Studio. You can use Compressor to get the ultimate bit rate to encode to MPEG-2 and use the entire 4.7GB DVD. Compressor provides many advanced features that help produce the highest-quality DVD possible.

Sending files directly from Final Cut Pro to Compressor

You can send sequences and clips directly from Final Cut Pro into Apple Compressor. You do this by right-clicking a sequence within the Browser window and selecting Export Using Compressor from the contextual menu.

Caution

If you are running a system with less than 4GB of RAM, save a QuickTime reference movie and then exit out of Final Cut Pro. Then import the QuickTime movie into Compressor for processing. I've found that by leaving both applications open, the conversion process takes considerably longer on computers with a limited amount of RAM.

When exporting a QuickTime movie, Final Cut Pro automatically creates a QuickTime reference movie if you uncheck the Make Movie Self-Contained check box (see figure 10.8). This dramatically decreases the export time, because Final Cut Pro only needs to export the audio portion of the movie. It references the original media using a QuickTime reference file. QuickTime reference movies only play on the computer that contains the referenced media. You cannot transfer a QuickTime reference movie to another computer to play the movie without the reference media.

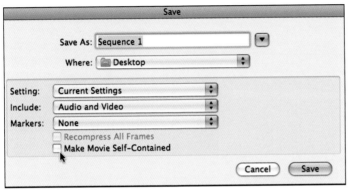

10.8 Leave the Make Movie Self-Contained check box unchecked to generate a QuickTime reference movie.

Using preset settings within Compressor

If you are new to Compressor, I recommend sticking with the default presets that are available to you. To create a DVD using the highest-quality preset, follow these steps:

1. **Either send a file directly into Compressor from Final Cut Pro, or manually open a file with Compressor.** If you choose to open a file manually, press the Add File button in the upper-left corner of the Compressor Batch window (see figure 10.9).

10.9 The Add File button in the Compressor Batch window.

2. **Navigate to the Settings tab and find the DVD: Best Quality setting.** The DVD: Best Quality setting is found by navigating through the various right-facing triangles to Apple ⇨ DVD ⇨ DVD: Best Quality 90 minutes.

3. **Drag the folder labeled 'DVD: Best Quality: 90 minutes' into the Batch window.** This folder contains the settings for both audio and video compression.

4. **Press the Submit button (see figure 10.10).** This begins the encode process.

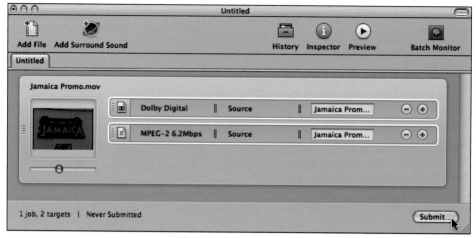

10.10 The Batch Monitor window.

Compressor starts to encode in the background. While Compressor works, you can add additional files for processing. You can also continue to work on other things while Compressor works in the background. The default location of the new file is the same location where the original file resides. When Compressor is finished encoding, you can use the newly encoded file directly in DVD Studio Pro. Because this file has already been encoded using Compressor, the DVD authoring process is much faster within DVD Studio Pro, as the file has already been encoded into the MPEG-2 format.

Using Compressor frame controls to increase quality

By creating a custom setting in Compressor, you are given access to the frame controls (see figure 10.11). The frame controls can increase the quality of compression. By using frame controls, you can obtain quality that has traditionally only been available to very expensive hardware-based real-time encoders. The only disadvantage is the amount of encoding time.

In order to use the frame controls, you must first duplicate an existing setting.

1. **Highlight the DVD: Best Quality 120 minutes setting within the Settings tab.**

2. **Click the Duplicate Selected Setting button in the upper-left corner of the Settings tab.** This places a duplicate copy of the best-quality DVD setting in the custom folder at the bottom of the list of settings. Click the right-facing disclosure triangle for the folder to display the audio and video settings. You only need to be concerned about the video settings; you can leave the audio settings alone.

3. **Double-click the MPG-2 5.- Mpbs 2 pass setting located inside the DVD: Best Quality folder.** The Inspector window appears.

4. **Click the Frame Controls button within the Inspector window.** To turn on the frame controls, click the asterisk button next to the Frame Controls setting. Then set the Frame Controls drop-down menu to On.

5. **There are several controls that you can adjust that will increase the quality of the final encode.** A popular setting is the ability to deinterlace video as Best (Motion compensated).

6. **At the top of the Inspector, give your new setting a name and description.**

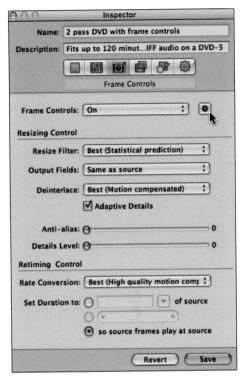

10.11 Frame controls with Apple Compressor.

Caution Using frame controls may dramatically affect the processing time required to encode your movie. It may also increase the size of the file. Bottom line, you need to experiment with the controls to determine which settings produce the best quality based on the amount of time that you have available for the program to encode the video.

Eliminate repetitive tasks using droplets

Any setting in Compressor can have a droplet created for automated use. Anyone who is not familiar with Compressor only needs to drop their movie file onto the droplet icon. That's it; Compressor does the rest based on the preconfigured settings of the droplet.

To create a droplet

1. **Highlight a setting within Compressor.**

2. **Click the Save Selection as Droplet button in the upper-left corner of the Settings tab (see figure 10.12).** I recommend saving the droplet directly to your Mac OS X desktop.

3. **You need only select where you want the droplet to be located and where the droplet should place the files it creates.**

Now you're golden! Anyone who needs to compress a high-quality DVD only needs to drag their finished movie onto the droplet (see figure 10.13). Compressor automatically opens and does the rest.

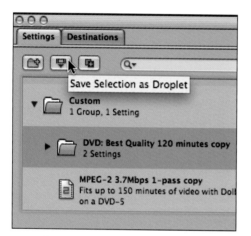

10.13 Dragging the movie file onto a droplet for automatic processing.

10.12 The Save Selection as Droplet button.

MPEG playback component for QuickTime

If you'd like the ability to play MPEG files directly within QuickTime, you need to download and install the MPEG playback component. You can purchase the playback component (or codec) directly from the Apple Web site at www.apple.com/quicktime/mpeg2/.

The MPEG-2 playback component supports playback for the following file types: .mpg, mpeg, .vob(2), .vro, .m2v, m2a, and m2s. Fortunately, you do not need the MPEG playback component to play MPEG-4 movie files.

Adding Chapter Points

If your final product is being distributed on DVD, you can use Final Cut Pro to add chapter points ahead of time. Chapter points are created by using markers within a sequence. Each marker is then assigned metadata that tells iDVD or DVD Studio Pro to create a chapter at that location on the DVD.

Genius

Using Final Cut Pro to add chapter markers can be a more precise way of adding chapters. If you choose to add chapters directly in DVD Studio Pro, they may be off by a frame or two because of the GOP structure implemented within MPEG-2 video. Placing a chapter marker forces DVD Studio Pro to create a chapter on a physical frame at the specified location by creating an 'I-Frame' within the GOP structure of the MPEG-2 file.

To add markers to a sequence, follow these steps:

1. **Within a finished sequence, press the M key twice at a point where you want a chapter.** Pressing the M key the first time adds the physical marker (see figure 10.14), and pressing it the second time brings forward the Edit Marker dialog.

10.14 Adding markers to a sequence.

2. **Click the Add Chapter Marker button (see figure 10.15).** This adds the required metadata to the marker in order to turn it into a DVD chapter. Click OK.

Caution

When adding a marker to a sequence, make sure that no clips are selected within the sequence. Otherwise, the marker will be embedded within a clip.

3. **Add additional markers throughout your sequence to represent chapter points by repeating steps 1 and 2.** If you decide to edit a marker, you can use keyboard shortcuts to jump to and from marker points. Then press the M key again to reopen the Marker dialog. Pressing Option+M moves the playhead indicator backward to the previous marker. Pressing Shift+M moves the playhead indicator forward to the next marker.

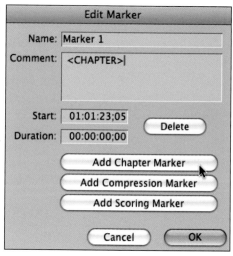

4. **Right-click your sequence that contains the chapter markers and select Export ⇨ QuickTime Movie from the contextual menu.** The Save dialog appears.

10.15 Adding chapter metadata to a marker.

5. **Click the Markers drop-down menu and select Chapter Markers (see figure 10.16).** Click the Save button. Final Cut Pro embeds the chapter markers directly into the exported sequence.

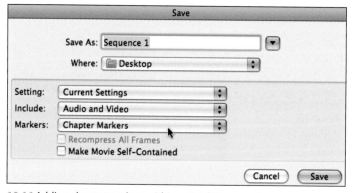

10.16 Adding chapter markers within a QuickTime movie.

You can now import your sequence into either iDVD or DVD Studio Pro, and the chapters are automatically created for you. Actually, all you need to do is drag your movie file directly into an iDVD theme (see figure 10.17). It's quite amazing!

Caution

Just make sure you don't drop your movie into a drop zone. Drop zones are for visual reference only.

10.17 Chapter markers added automatically within iDVD.

Adding Compression Markers

You can add compression markers to your sequence the same way you add chapter markers. Just like a chapter marker, a compression marker tells DVD Studio Pro to create an I-Frame at a specified location. The only difference is that a compression marker doesn't leave a physical chapter point. So you may ask yourself, what's the big deal?

Remember, an I-Frame is part of the GOP structure that makes up an MPEG-2 file. An I-Frame is the only frame in the GOP structure that isn't predictive. In other words, it's a full frame. Well, it turns out that cross-dissolves and other complex frames do not compress very well, especially if the frame ends up being a P- or B-frame.

You can add a compression marker as a way of telling DVD Studio Pro to compress a particular frame as an I-Frame. This increases the quality of compression when encountering a complex frame. Otherwise, if a dissolve lands too far from the nearest I-Frame, the quality tends to be very poor.

You may run into a situation where you have both chapter markers and compression markers. If this is the case, make sure you choose DVD Studio Pro Markers from the drop-down menu when exporting your final sequence. This menu selection is set to include both chapter markers and compression markers.

Output Settings for the Web

The most popular and efficient way to submit your film to festivals is now through a Web site. YouTube is another method that many people are employing to post video to the Web.

The important thing to understand is that the video you create with Final Cut Pro will be recompressed before making it to the Internet. A popular codec for producing Web content is MPEG-4. One way to produce MPEG-4 videos that has very positive results is to right-click a sequence within the Browser window and choose Export ➪ QuickTime Conversion from the contextual menu. You now have the ability to select iPod or iPhone from the Format drop-down menu. iPod and iPhone videos are both encoded using the MPEG-4 codec.

How to make your iPod videos look fantastic

iPod video is typically MPEG-4, which is what makes the files so small. The compression to MPEG-4 reduces the quality of the image. QuickTime movies that have not been compressed to MPEG-4 can be played on an iPod — they just take up a lot more space. If you are using the iPod to play back to a projector for a presentation, you may want to choose something other than MPEG-4.

Important export settings for iPhone video clips

When you are exporting video for the iPhone, the obvious choice would be to export with the iPhone setting. By selecting the iPod setting instead of the iPhone setting, the increased quality is noticeable. The file size is about twice as much as with the iPhone setting, but it is still quite small.

Genius

Output to Tape

This topic is quickly becoming obsolete. That being said, you may still encounter a job that needs to go back to videotape. If this is the case, Final Cut Pro provides a fantastic feature called Print to Video (see figure 10.18). It contains all the parameters that you need when laying back a sequence to videotape.

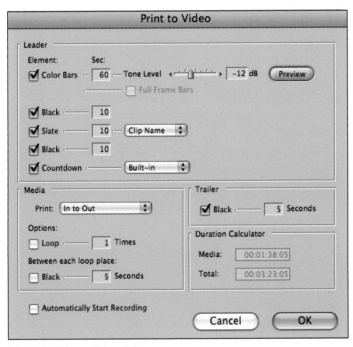

10.18 The Print to Video dialog.

To lay back a sequence to tape

1. **Highlight your sequence in the Browser window.**

2. **Click File ⇨ Print to video.** A Print to Video dialog appears.

3. **Choose the appropriate settings within the Print to Video dialog, and click OK.**

Caution

Notice that there is an Automatically Start Recording check box in the Print to Video dialog. I don't recommend turning this option on unless you are absolutely certain you are printing to the correct tape. All too often, I've accidentally had a tape already in the tape machine, not realizing that I was about to record over it.

How Can I Benefit from Media Management?

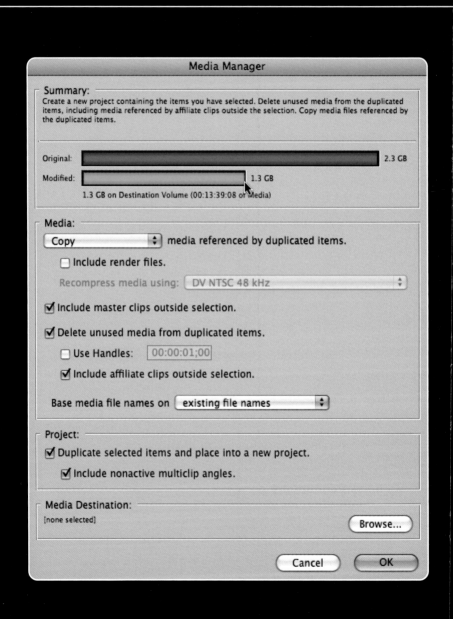

Good media management in Final Cut Pro is not difficult to maintain. However, it does require some thought in terms of your editing workflow. A large part of managing media can actually be done outside of Final Cut Pro.

Organizing Media

Whenever you import a file into Final Cut Pro, it knows where it came from and maintains a linked relationship in terms of referencing the media. What happens all too often is that files get reorganized on the hard drive after they have been imported into Final Cut Pro. The link is then broken, and files may appear offline (see figure 11.1).

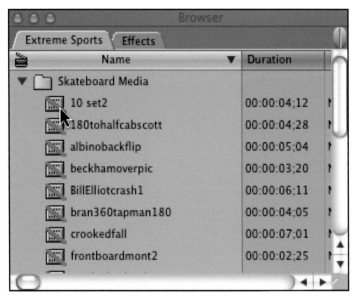

11.1 Media offline in the Browser window.

The key to staying organized is to keep all of your media elements in one location. At first, this might seem relatively simple. How hard can it be to organize a few items? Because you'll be using the entire Final Cut Studio to build your project, you'll typically end up with elements from Final Cut Pro, Motion, LiveType, Soundtrack Pro, DVD Studio Pro, Apple Compressor, and Color. Then throw in a graphic or two from Photoshop, and you'll quickly understand why it's important to stay organized. When it comes time to archive or save your media, you'll understand why it's a great idea to have everything stored in one location that's properly organized.

Managing the main media folder

So where should you store this master folder? One solution is to use the folder that the Log and Capture tool or Log and Transfer tool creates. Final Cut Pro automatically creates a folder called Capture Scratch, and inside this folder it creates another folder that matches the name of your project (see figure 11.2). These folders are automatically created as soon as you record your first clip. This is something that happens automatically and cannot be changed.

11.2 Capture Scratch folder.

Because these folders are going to be created automatically, you might as well create subfolders that include all your external elements. This way, when you archive or manage all of your data, you'll be sure to have all your material.

Final Cut Pro also automatically creates a series of folders that include Audio Render Files, Autosave Vault, Render Files, Thumbnail, and Waveform Cache Files. Each folder contains a list of folders that match your project name. The critical folder is the one labeled Capture Scratch. The contents of the other folders, with the exception of the Autosave Vault, can be recreated.

Genius

You can import folders and files directly from the Mac OS X Finder into the Final Cut Pro Browser window. Therefore, if you create a template of what your typical Project Folder will look like, and always start with that, your life will be much easier.

Using the Mac OS X Finder

Having an organized project folder in the Finder can be just as important as having everything in the Browser window. You can think of the Browser window and Mac OS X Finder as one and the same (see figure 11.3).

Each project may have some different subfolders, but starting with a template helps you maintain good media management. Once you have populated the subfolders of your Project Folder, it is

225

time to import it into Final Cut Pro. Any empty folders do not import, and all others import as folders and subfolders. Personally, I only bring my audio and video into the Finder because everything else changes throughout the project.

By creating this Project Folder structure once and saving it with empty folders, you can start from it each time you start a project. By preparing an organized project folder, you keep yourself disciplined not to put files where they don't belong. Whenever you need something for a Final Cut Pro project, you can go straight to the Finder.

For example, your LiveType project folder may have one or two titles that you are going to reuse from a previous project, or titles you may have already created for this project.

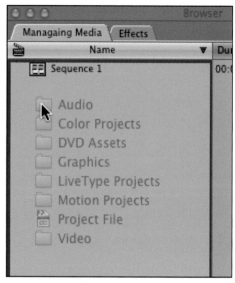

11.3 Importing files from the Finder into the Browser window.

Genius

You can import media directly from the Mac OS X Finder window to a Final Cut Pro sequence, which bypasses the Browser window altogether. If you think about it, the only advantage of using the Browser window is that you are able to mark in and out points for various clip elements.

You may find it easier to import LiveType projects directly into the Final Cut Pro timeline (see figure 11.4). You won't be able to drag the LiveType project icon directly from the LiveType interface until you have saved your project. Make sure you are saving your LiveType project to its correct folder to stay organized.

There are some great previewing capabilities in the Finder that are not available in the

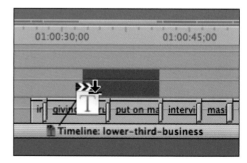

11.4 Importing a LiveType project directly into the Final Cut Pro timeline.

Browser window. When you are parked on a file, pressing the Space bar displays a small Quicklook viewer of any movie, image, or audio file (see figure 11.5). As you move down through the list with the arrow keys, it automatically plays each file. Pressing the Space bar again closes the Quicklook viewer. You can then drag the file you need directly to the Timeline window within Final Cut Pro.

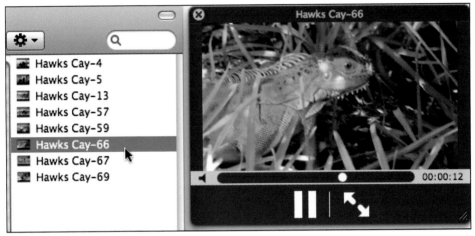

11.5 Quicklook functionality in Mac OS X Leopard.

Note

The Quicklook functionality requires Mac OS 10.5 (Leopard) or higher.

Managing clips in the Browser window

It's critical to understand that clips within the Browser window are essentially pointers to the original files located on your hard drive. That's why it may make sense to manage the majority of your media directly from the Mac OS X Finder, as that's where the media actually resides.

When you rename clips within the Browser window, note that Final Cut Pro does not rename the files that those clips are pointing to. This means that the clips in the Browser window will not match the referenced media on the hard drive. This can lead to a media management disaster in the future.

Renaming clips

Fortunately, there are two functions that allow you to reestablish the naming structure so that the clips in the Browser window match the names of the clips that they are referencing. You have two choices:

- **Clip to Match File.** This updates filenames within the Browser window to match the name of the media file on a hard drive.

- **File to Match File.** This updates the media filenames on the hard drive to match the names of clips within the Browser window. Because you'll be working with and organizing clips within the Browser window, this is a more common choice.

To update media files on your hard drive to match the names of clips within Final Cut Pro, follow these steps:

1. **Select a group of clips within the Browser window.**

2. **Right-click any of the selected clips' icons to reveal the contextual menu, and select Rename ⇨ File to Match Clip (see figure 11.6).** Mac OS X warns you that you are about to modify a source file. Click OK to continue.

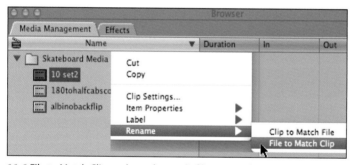

11.6 File to Match Clip updates the mediafile on your hard drive to match.

Using subclips in the Browser window

Another good strategy to manage media is to work with large single clips that are divided into subclips. Renaming subclips does not affect the referenced media.

To create subclips from a larger clip, follow these steps:

1. **Load the clip into the Viewer window by double-clicking it.**

2. **Mark in and out points for a specified area of the clip.**

3. **Click Modify ⇨ Make Subclip.** A subclip is created in the Browser window. You can also use the keyboard shortcut ⌘+U to create a subclip.

4. **Repeat this process for each subclip that you want to create.**

By renaming subclips (see figure 11.7), you won't need to worry about renaming clips in the Browser window to match the referenced media on your hard drive. All the subclips will point back to the original master clip.

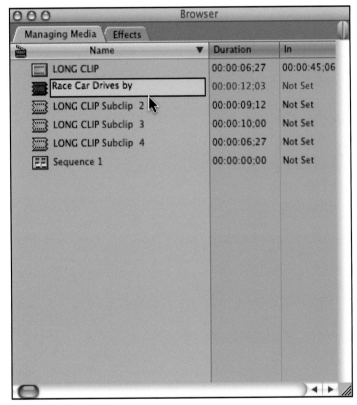

11.7 Renaming subclips.

Genius

You can use the DV Start/Stop Detection functionality to automatically create subclips based on the start-stop marks that are placed within the media during the shooting process. For more information on DV Start/Stop Detection, see Chapter 3.

Using the Render Manager

When you perform a render function in Final Cut Pro, a Render Files folder is placed on your hard drive automatically, and is based on your scratch disk settings. Separate folders are created for video and audio renders. From an organizational point of view, I recommend that you keep the render folders for audio and video on the same hard drive as your video elements.

You can access the Render Manager by selecting Tools ⇨ Render Manager (see figure 11.8). The Render Manager displays all the current projects that contain rendered media. Each render folder is broken down based on individual projects that they belong to. To remove rendered files, place a check mark in the Remove column for each folder you want to delete.

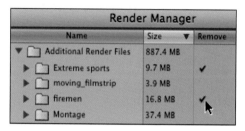

11.8 The Render Manager.

For the most part, it is relatively safe to delete all the render files when you are finished with a particular project, as they generally just sit there and take up space. In a worst-case scenario, you'll have to rerender everything.

Caution — If you delete all your rendered files and then choose to perform an Undo function that references a previous render file, you will need to rerender the effect.

You may run into a situation where you spend hours waiting for your system to render a complex effect. If something changes within your sequence, you may find yourself having to rerender the composite. This can be frustrating, especially if the effect is finished and it suddenly becomes unrendered.

You can navigate to the Render Files folder on your Capture Scratch drive and find the actual render file (see figure 11.9). Move this file to another location and place it back into your sequence. This is essentially the same thing as a video mixdown. Just make sure you keep a copy of all the original video layers in case you need to change something.

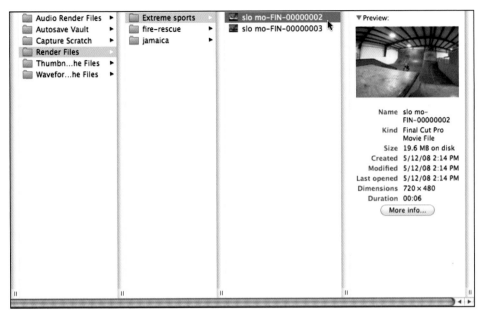

11.9 Stealing a render file to use within a Final Cut Pro project.

Using the Media Manager

The Media Manager is a tool that allows you to manage content based on timecode information embedded within all your clips. You can use this tool to consolidate media that only contains the necessary media to play back your sequence.

Caution Be extremely careful when using the Media Manager; certain functions are irreversible.

The Media Manager is a fantastic tool for dealing with large projects that contain a lot of content. I recommend using this tool if you are working with narrative-style or documentary-style shows. For the Media Manager to work correctly, it's extremely important that all of the captured clips contain the original timecode information from their source.

The Media Manager only works correctly with clips that contain timecode information. Clips that do not contain timecode information are not included as part of the managed process. Any elements that are converted from non-timecode sources won't work with the Media Manager. This would include media that is imported from an audio CD, DVD, VHS tape, or Web movie.

Consolidating media

To consolidate a sequence using the Media Manager, follow these steps:

1. **Highlight your finished sequence within the Browser window.**

2. **Select File ⇨ Media Manager.**

3. **Set the Media drop-down menu to Copy media referenced by duplicate items.**

4. **Click the Delete unused media from duplicated items option.**

5. **Click the Duplicate selected items and place into new project option.**

6. **Click the Browse button to set a new media location for the new files that will be created.**

   Before continuing, pay special attention to the green media graph at the top of the Media Manager dialog (see figure 11.10). This graph gives you a summary of what is about to happen. If the graph doesn't make sense in terms of how much media will be retained, do not continue. Stop and research the problem, because depending on the options that you have selected, this process may be irreversible.

7. **Click OK to consolidate the media into a new project.**

If the Duplicate selected items and place into new project option is selected and you'd like to keep additional media outside of the selected sequence, click the Include master clips outside selection check box. This creates a new project with clips required to play your sequence, plus additional areas that have in and out points for clips in your project.

The Use Handles option provides additional media on each side of a clip once the media is consolidated. This gives you the ability to trim clips beyond their original edit point based on the amount of handles that you have specified.

Recompressing media

You can perform additional functions with the Media Manager, such as recompressing or transcoding media to a different format. There are some limitations for transcoding between certain codecs or frame rates. For example, you cannot convert NTSC media to PAL media. The frame size would change, but the frame rate would remain the same.

Media Manager

Summary:
Create a new project containing the items you have selected. Include active Multiclip angles only. Delete unused media from the duplicated items. Copy media files referenced by the duplicated items.

Original: `[██████████████████████]` 445.5 MB

Modified: `[████]` 112.7 MB

112.7 MB on Destination Volume (00:00:31:26 of Media)

Media:

`[ Copy ▲▼ ]` media referenced by duplicated items.

☐ Include render files.

Recompress media using: `[ DV NTSC 48 kHz ▲▼ ]`

☑ Include master clips outside selection.

☑ Delete unused media from duplicated items.

   ☐ Use Handles: `[ 00:00:01;00 ]`

   ☐ Include affiliate clips outside selection.

Base media file names on `[ existing file names ▲▼ ]`

Project:

☑ Duplicate selected items and place into a new project.

   ☐ Include nonactive multiclip angles.

Media Destination:

[none selected]   (Browse...)

(Cancel)   (OK)

11.10 The Media Manager dialog.

Moving media with the Media Manager

Moving media can be a dangerous process. I recommend that you copy the media first, and make sure it plays. Then go back and delete the old media. That being said, you can certainly use the Media Manager to move and manage your media without having to copy it first (see figure 11.11).

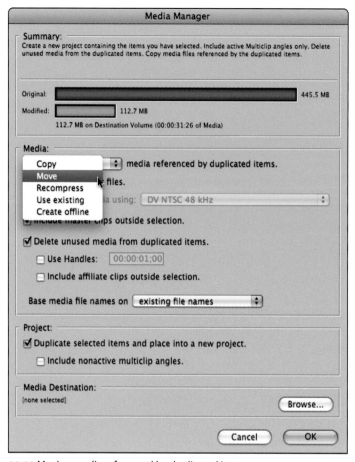

11.11 Moving media referenced by duplicated items.

When moving media, you must check the Delete unused media from duplicated items option. Otherwise, you'll simply be copying the media. When moving media, Final Cut Pro always includes additional media for clips that have in and out points that are being used in your sequence. If you do not want the extra media, you must remove any in or out points for all your clips that are associated with that particular project.

You can clear all the in and out points for a series of clips by highlighting them all within the Browser window, right-clicking inside the In or Out column, and selecting Clear In or Clear Out from the contextual menu (see figure 11.12).

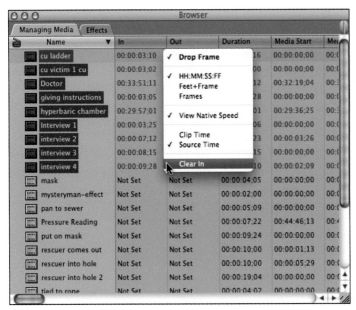

11.12 Clearing in and out points for multiple clips.

Note The only difference between moving media and using existing media is that the physical location where the media is stored will not change when managing existing media.

Creating offline media

Creating offline media is essentially the same as deleting a project's Capture Scratch folder on the hard drive. The one difference is that you can preset sequences to a different resolution. This option is really only practical to those users who are working on feature films or long-format documentaries where it is not practical to record all the media at its fullest resolution. The basic workflow is to capture all the media at a lower resolution, and then edit the entire sequence. When you are done, you can recapture all the media at its highest resolution based on timecode values for all the clips.

To recapture a sequence that is offline:

1. **Highlight the finished sequence in the Browser window.**
2. **Select File ⇨ Batch Capture.** A batch capture window appears, asking for the original source material to be re-captured.

Target Mode

All Macs have the ability to start up in Target mode. This means that you can configure your Mac as a hard drive, which can then be plugged into another computer. This makes it incredibly easy to copy media between your computer and another system. Better yet, if you are a MacBook or MacBook Pro owner, you can configure your laptop as a hard drive that runs on its own battery!

To do this, you need to completely power down your Mac. Hold down the T key when you start your computer. The computer eventually displays a FireWire symbol on the screen. This means that it is ready to be hooked up to another computer using a FireWire cable. The computer mounts just like any other drive on the other computer's desktop. You can then copy media between the computers.

Archiving Media

With the introduction of tapeless technologies, the concept of archiving media is changing. It was common in the past to archive media to tape. Today, the process is reversed; we are now archiving taped data to hard disks.

Currently the best choice for archiving large amounts of data is to back up the information to a low-cost hard drive. Hard-drive capacities now exceed 1 terabyte, which represents 1,000 giga-bytes of information. You don't necessarily need a high-speed drive, but the speed of the drive affects how long it takes to copy the media.

If you are archiving relatively small amounts of media, you can burn the data to a DVD. Keep in mind that a standard single-layer DVD only contains enough space for 4.7GB of data. A Blu-Ray DVD provides enough space for 25GB of data. You can also purchase dual-layer disks, which provide twice that capacity.

Caution Tapeless technologies are quickly replacing mechanical machines that deal with tape. Budget for additional storage to make archived copies of your media as a secure backup.

There is an argument that if you are using Final Cut Pro for a feature-length film, you could implement a method of working with low-resolution material to save disk space. But again, even feature films are slowly beginning to adopt digital video as their method of shooting.

A lot of Final Cut Pro editors spend way too much time recapturing or looking for lost data when they could have simply invested in a couple of terabytes of hard drive storage to avoid all their problems. In the past, storage was incredibly expensive. Now, with a few exceptions, you can simply go out and purchase enough storage to complete the job. Then, you can either archive your material or delete it when you are finished.

Index

The Genius is in.

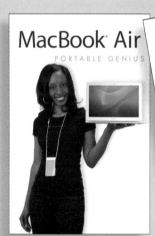

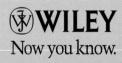